BETTER HIRES
FULLY STAFFED

A Medical Device Manager's Guide to Hiring Top Talent
In order to Build a High-Performance Sales Team,
Increase Revenue and Minimize Turnover

Anthony Cochrane

Copyright 2018 Anthony Cochrane

Edited by:
Sandi Masori
Navid Aberg

ISBN 13: 978-1790392742

ACKNOWLEDGEMENTS

Each person that you encounter in life can either be an example or a warning. It has taken me a long time to surround myself with those who exemplify the upstanding individual that I strive to become.

Ryan Belford introduced my company to recruiting for the big leagues. When I met Ryan, he had an interest in what I was doing and gave me the shot to recruit on an open position for Bard in October of 2016. We filled the difficult position that had been open for a couple months, and are forever grateful for this initial opportunity as we now partner with every division of Bard/BD.

Scott Herron inspired me to build a recruiting company by recruiting me! Scott shared his recruiting and healthcare knowledge from his background at J&J. He gave me an opportunity to learn and grow, and it worked out great. His company continues to thrive, and his consistently positive and helpful outlook continues to inspire me.

Landmark Worldwide was the training program that motivated me to create the life that I knew I wanted. It helped me to break out of my shell and take risks like starting National Source Recruiting. It helped me orchestrate personal and professional changes in my life to improve my health and deepen my relationships with each person I know. It even led to me organizing a big beach volleyball tournament called Digs for Dogs for charity, which I thought would be very hard to do, and through which I carried self-doubt. Though afterwards and with thousands raised for a local animal charity, the boost in confidence was amazing.

To my wife, Debbie, who never ceases to inspire me. She is spontaneous, passionate, and on fire with everything that she touches. The deeper I know her and love her, the more that I hope her qualities rub off on me. This book would not have been written without her, and my company and feelings of fulfilment would not exist without her.

I am in debt to all hiring managers and candidates that I have worked with over the years. One manager who contributed to this book said, "It's about finding good people." This is exactly the case. I have been more than privileged to partner with these managers and many others who I have met in person. These individuals have been **extremely** helpful in guiding me to help grow their personal teams with their amazing feedback and industry expertise. Although some are newer to management, their insight from years of success in the field and as managers has been a profound resource.

Royce Carter

Ryan Silsbe

Mike Padgett

Jason Nelson

Paul DiMartino

Greg Genoa

Brett Johnston

Mark Hayward

TABLE OF CONTENTS

MY WHY

It is June 30th 2004. As the bagpipes play Amazing Grace, it hits me so hard that I can't hold back the tears. My closest relatives lift a casket with my father's body into a hearse. He is going home, and I never got the opportunity to say goodbye.

Exactly one week before, on the evening of June 23rd, 2004 I was driving to my family's home in the Santa Cruz mountains. I was 18 and it was the summer after graduating high school. I had just seen my girlfriend at the time. As I approached the house a few extra lights were on. I was late, but not so late where they were organizing a search party for me. As I walk in the door, I see some of my relatives and then, my mom. I see a sadness painted on her face, in her eyes, as she walks over and hugs me. Coming from a mother who always showed love, I knew something was very wrong. She said, "your father has been in an accident." I knew at that moment that I would never see him again.

The day before, my father left with the old truck to my grand-ma's house in the country. At first light, he drove to Yosemite where he planned to summit world famous Half Dome. He fell near the summit, over 300 feet off the granite face of the mountain. A hiker that day reported a man on the trail complaining of chest pain. This was my father. A ranger was called to the scene, and his body was medavaced out by helicopter. My sister-in-law is an emergency nurse in one of those rescue helicopters today in the Bay Area. And, while there was no rescue that day, there are countless rescues from emergency helicopters and in hospitals each hour of every day.

It is my honor and privilege to be a vital part of placing the top sales professionals into the dream career of medical device sales. Here, they are trusted advisors to the most capable doctors, nurses, and clinicians so that more lives can be saved and improved.

I wanted to be there to support my mom and sister, and was very close to not leaving for college a few months later. Now looking back, making the choice to go out on my own, and eventually start National Source Recruiting has propelled me to the goal of helping thousands of candidates break into medical device sales to help others, and earn more at the same time. I am extremely passionate about pursuing this goal during my lifetime.

INTRODUCTION

Two years ago, I started working with a medical device manager from a large client. We were connected through many other managers in the division; he was recently promoted and also inherited a vacancy.

He had worked with another recruiter for a few weeks on the opening. That firm claimed that the well was dry, and there were only a couple of candidates in the interview process. When we spoke live, this manager explained to me his frustrations. And this was just three weeks after they had started interviewing.

He was currently balancing the workload of managing, selling and interviewing candidates multiple times a week. This extra workload was wearing on him. Besides having a young family and other obligations, he was being spread very thin.

He said that HR supplied candidates, but not at a steady flow and the quality was not there. For example, some were not currently in sales, others had been at multiple jobs each year since college, and there were many that simply were not a good fit. Candidates were being funneled to him from the recruiting agency and HR infrequently, and they were not qualified. He was looking for the hungry rep with a couple years of sales under their belt, looking for not only a bump in pay, but also a move to a dream industry.

This is the story that we hear all too often. The current recruiting agency and HR are both not delivering talent. The cost is stress on you as the manager, and time wasted on both yours and the candidate's behalf, and after all that - no hire.

I recently had a conversation with a VP at a large San Diego-based medical device company. For a couple years, their sales force has been on a downward spiral. The company had previously relied on their name recognition in a couple of their divisions to stay competitive. This VP works with many of the managers and told me about their competitors, and how his company could not poach any other device reps because his company really would not complete a thorough sourcing process, and pushed candidates to interview who applied to their posts. While a name and reputation can in fact attract talent, he acknowledged that the company has had no actual sourcing process. We will talk about this process in depth.

Their talent acquisition team does not reach out to passive candidates, and typically sends candidates without relevant sales experience and even those who are not a fit. HR cites that they are doing their job by supplying the managers with the applicants who applied. This is not the process we recommend.

I am a big advocate for additions on LinkedIn. When there are job ads posted on LinkedIn and other job sites, buzz is generated. You would be surprised, though, that the majority of these high-energy job posts do not get a lot of views and attention (i.e. "likes" and QUALIFIED applicants). There needs to be a more proactive approach.

Farming the current candidate pool in your network as a manager is mediocre, and if you land a good hire then you just got lucky.

The solution is a lengthy process called sourcing, and it can be broken down to a science. The entire candidate pool is searched, leaving no stone unturned, and you ultimately find your next star.

If these frustrations sound anything like what you are going through as a manager, worry no more! The process I will take you through in this book encompasses the sourcing steps to success that we take with each open position. This all happens behind the scenes, with your guidance leading the charge in the initial discovery call. Proceeding this way the magic happens, and those candidates magically "appear" in a submittal email to you, even though they typically do not have their resumes on any job boards.

There will be no sifting through email after email of unqualified candidates. This will ultimately save you precious time, so that you can focus more on being a team leader.

The process of how a resourceful recruiting agency finds top talent involves:

- Calling resumes off the bat of matching candidates
- Reaching out to existing contacts in and around the location (relocation candidates if you are open to it)
- Calling reps from our lists of candidates in the city
- Asking all contacts we know in the surrounding area for <u>referrals</u>
- Adding reps on LinkedIn from target company lists
- Sending an InMail via LinkedIn to passive candidates who are in the network but are not our connections, or who do not add us on LinkedIn
- Cold-calling rosters of companies

- Dialing 1-800 numbers of our target companies
- Dropping in to physically call on San Diego Enterprise branches and ADP offices with the goal of at least a couple of cards
- Working with regional recruiters around the county who have a deep talent pool

The process is lengthy, but is not something you have to work on! Each step is very necessary and one hundred percent worthwhile in finding your new top teammate. Our goal is to place someone who will be with you and the company for decades to come.

I speak to candidates for a couple hours a day. Candidates will often ask about relocation roles, and roles in different expertises. If they are in clinical sales, they will ask about sales rep roles. If they are sales reps, they will ask about management roles. I agree that anything is possible, but typically you are looking for a rep for a rep role, or a trainer for a trainer role, etc. If you would be open to an associate rep to fill your territory manager position, then this completely works.

For example, on a couple occasions we have received manager roles where they were looking at outside candidates. The majority of the time they should hire internally for these roles. The applicant works for the company, and has already sold the devices and been a success. The odds of them building on this foundation are much better than someone who has to learn the products, company culture, nuances with a new company and ramping up, etc. (because they came from another company) AND also has to learn to lead!

You would most likely want management for a management position so that the new hire is up to speed on successfully managing teams. With this background, they are likely to jump in and make a huge splash. While they may have different call-points and some devices to study-up on, they have the leadership part down already. It is infrequent to have a management opening not requiring leadership experience. A field trainer is often skilled in field rides and interviewing, and sometimes will be the next best fit for management positions.

The relocation game is one that frequently comes up over phone conversations. The candidate will live for example in Los Angeles, but be open to Seattle and San Francisco roles. As a recruiting agency, we are paid when we provide just A+ candidates. You would rather see a Sally that lives in your open territory, say Seattle, than a Sally who has to fly in for multiple interviews from Las Vegas, and also has to create a new life and pay for multiple trips before even landing the job!

We are not paid for a huge number of weaker candidates. I say weak not referring to their skill level; the candidate fitting your requisition is a given. Their location, however is a key factor and relocation candidates filling the role are less attractive.

We have to explain to the relocation candidate that if there are similar candidates interviewing who already live locally, they will land the role one in ten times or less all other things being equal. The reasoning for this is that for most major device manufacturers, there are multiple face-to-faces sometimes at the drop of a hat. There may be a couple days' notice, or up to a week or two at the very maximum. There can also be a field ride, and a final interview in or near the city where the opening is. Even with just three or four steps in person, six to eight separate plane tickets can get expensive. Add in food, a rental car or Uber and taxi services, and opportunity cost for them taking multiple days off their current role, and it makes zero sense!

When it is laid out that way, the candidate will usually agree that yes, they will not be able to head up to Seattle four separate times, sometimes with a few days' notice. They are currently employed, and would be jeopardizing their current job and also spending a ton on flights with <u>no guarantee</u> of a new job.

When switching roles or hats in the device world, a candidate is better off staying with their existing company. Performers build rapport with their superiors, team, and all those around them. There is no shortage of people willing to vouch for them. When a clinical rep has shining endorsements like these and great numbers in their existing roles, they can let it be known that they want a sales rep role within their current organization.

On the other hand, when a candidate tells me over the phone that they would like me to find them a rep role a few states away, years ago I used to mistakenly say "will do." I would do my best and often land them interviews. It has come with experience, and frequently sending the wrong candidates that I have become more clear on what the right candidates are.

From sending candidates like this in, feedback I would typically get from a manager would be, "I would like someone currently in outside sales or device sales already." To the relocation candidate submittal, they are just not an "A" or even a "B" candidate - not because of their performance, but due to them not being able to interview and the odds of them pulling off relocation interviews.

A common concern that comes up is a network when moving to a new city. In this day and age, wanderlust is very common. The Millennials (myself and many of us included) are the "experience generation" stereotyped by frequent travel, experiences and time off. All these are wonderful things. However, when landing a new device role, inability to do what it takes to succeed and work the long hours and not take off frequently is paramount.

On the flip-side, high performers need time for family, vacations, hobbies, and ways of coping with medical device jobs that can be very stressful. The thing about a candidate wanting to live in a new city means a new network, and group of people. The odds of them being successful there are lower than in their current city.

Imagine moving alone to a new city without friends, family or any contacts. Could you make it? If you are reading this, you're probably a success in sales and relationship building, and could. Would it be easier to make it in your current city? The answer to this one would be "yes" just about every time.

The necessity for a great recruiting agency becomes obvious when others will begin to look for candidates themselves. I had a client who would search for an hour or two in the evenings for reps online. This manager enjoyed it, and liked learning about different companies and would run them by me frequently.

With sourcing, it can be hard when someone has a network of 100 or even 500 on LinkedIn. They can only see their contacts' contacts, and no more "degrees" than that. On the flipside, in my 20,000 network, I can see their connections, and all of the additional connections on LinkedIn because of the high-level of accounts that we have.

Other confusing factors can be finding out what job title is really a sales rep. For example, with Altria, a distribution company for tobacco products, a Unit Manager is a promoted sales rep. At Enterprise, an Account Specialist is in sales, whereas an Account Representative is in a call center taking incoming calls.

Imagine contacting an Account Representative on your own, pitching them your position, and a step or two into the process you realize they are an inside sales rep (more of a reservationist). Your time and theirs was wasted. This is where we fill in.

Going back to the DIY manager. He did not want to pay to subscribe to job boards, and I don't blame him. Paying for outdated resumes of candidates that are interviewing at every company under the sun is a waste of money.

This manager was building their contacts on LinkedIn. When you have a couple hundred LinkedIn contacts, and start to increase that number, you start to see other connections who are second or third degree. You may be able to see them, but cannot add them. This is when "InMail's" come into place. If you do not want to pay the thousands per year for the ability to inmail, then you can try to find their name and then cold-call the sales office of their organization for their number.

The manager told me that after a couple weeks of doing this (because he was not satisfied with the candidates being supplied by HR and his current recruiter), he had identified a couple candidates but could not even add them on LinkedIn. He was stuck, and would rather be doing his current job of being a leader and manager!

Do not put yourself in this position. While it seems intuitive to go find your new superstar yourself, there is a reason that companies use recruiting agencies and have HR departments. I have now worked successfully with that manager for over two years. It costs you nothing to use a recruiting agency, and the only regret you will have is not signing on sooner!

THE TEAM

Now that you know my deepest personal motivators for writing *Better Hires,* I can tell you that the best things come from collaboration. Teams are the effective units for selling medical devices. When I meet with or interact with medical device management, the team is constantly being discussed. The team is dynamic - growing and hiring, sometimes holding or even downsizing due to instruction from corporate. The individual members create the success exemplified by the leader. A full team is one prepared to tackle a high market share and be very effective. Each individual sits in his or her proper seat on the bus. To continue this culture, a new hire needs to be right. The rep with the exact qualities and coachability needs to be found.

On a typical medical device sales team, there are about eight to twelve members including a couple of reps in training or associate reps, a handful or more reps, potentially one to two clinical reps, a trainer and a manager who is also in the field. Most managers take a hands-on approach and still carry out sales successfully since they have been there and know best practices to consulting with and selling into healthcare. Many times the reps on a team have been there for a decade, or even more. The newer reps in training are called associate reps or associate territory managers.

Titles can get to be confusing. With some companies, for example, sales reps are called District Managers or Area Sales Managers. Territory Manager, Sales Representative, and Consultant are all more intuitive titles for a sales rep.

The associate rep positions are ground-level roles, where new hires are learning the ropes in thorough training programs both inside and in the field. The most successful associate reps are coachable, but also have outside sales experience under their belts, so they have a certain amount of selling already trained into them. To find the strongest hire for your team, it is recommended to hire reps from a sales "cold-calling" role with a minimum of six months, up to one or even two years of experience before breaking into an associate role. When a rep works for a large company with great sales and corporate training, on-going training, who is also tracked and provided with their sales rankings and percentages, they are setting themselves up for medical device sales.

Reps who go to work with companies such as ADP, Cintas, and Enterprise Rent-a-Car will have training from day one. They are being trained not only in sales, but also in customer service and how to run their "own business." These companies pride themselves on corporate training. When you hire a rep from a larger company, they will usually have some sales training at corporate, online training modules, in-office training regularly, etc. This can be a HUGE asset! When they transition over to your team they may not sell exactly the same, but they will have some common ground that transfers over. These reps may be trained to call on customers in a couple zip codes, and maybe even a couple states. They will have experience with varying levels of autonomy.

Frequently, reps at these companies have a branch meeting in the morning. Sometimes they have to also check-in at the end of the day. The road warrior sales reps that may sell payroll, to wine and spirits, to copy and print solutions, can cover a larger territory. For these reps, they might check into the office once or twice a week after showing steady success. These encounters will be for training, to touch base and also sometimes to even collect product and paperwork.

These types of "entry" business-to-business positions give a solid foundation when looking for an associate sales rep. I highly recommend this and find that ninety percent of the hires that we place on teams like yours come from these types of backgrounds.

If a rep does well a few years into outside sales roles. They will also have input in hiring. When this insight is given, they will interview other reps, help hire, and learn what types of qualities make a successful sales rep. At this point, they are even more savvy and can do better in interviews themselves. They can anticipate the types of behavioral questions they will be asked and will perform better in role-play scenarios during interviews. Promotions to roles where candidates interview others and great sales numbers speak for themselves.

Cold-calling can either make someone realize they are not cut out for sales, or make them understand they can earn as much as they desire and build their own future. For those in the second bucket, they are built for medical device sales.

When the associate rep is hired, they become part of a team which already has a culture and has worked well together. During the interview process there is often a step or even multiple steps for integration. The associate is usually well trained in sales, and can jump in and make an impact. These associates will have extensive training at corporate, at-home study, computer modules, and frequent field training with other reps and managers. All of these steps set them up with the best chances of success. The goal is to have them on the team for many years. They are being groomed to be successful associates, learning how the sales cycle works, how to support other reps, and how they will successfully manage a quota and be a top performer driving revenue as they transition over into a sales rep role.

Copy Job?

Ricoh is a very large copy, print and IT solutions company. When I graduated college, I landed a job with Ricoh. The manager said I would report to the office every day for a meeting, hit the phones and then attend appointments I had set for myself, and even go business-to-business knocking on doors. At the end of the day, we would finish with a debrief at the office around 5:30PM. This is a pure hunter sales job. The copy and print industry is a declining industry, as some of the large companies such as Lanier, Pitney Bowes, Xerox, etc. have vanished or gotten much smaller in recent years. The job scared me, and I was offered the position. They said go home and think if this type of tough job could work for me. I did not take the job. Now that I am a decade out of college, I finally have begun to realize that very scary things can sometimes be good! I didn't take the role but have high respect for those who are gutsy enough to work them.

I did land a job in sales through some colleagues I knew from school. One of them had a friend who started a company called Spott.com. They were a startup very similar to Groupon with the exception that some of the proceeds would go to various charities. As a sales rep, I would travel around San Diego with an iPad and set up Groupon-like deals with local businesses. I enjoyed the downtown office views, and also getting to know the different neighborhoods and businesses, restaurants, and activities (most that I was unaware of). Groupon typically takes half of the proceeds from a "deal", and the deal already cuts the company's prices in half. Our site would take a quarter portion typically. If we brought in new customers who cared about charities, the idea is that they were a different demographic.

Since your new hire will be in outside sales, we recommend a well-trained outside sales rep that brings coachability, a great sales track record, and who also strongly checks all the boxes during your interview process.

HIRING CHALLENGES

From surveying your colleagues in management, here is the list of the most desirable qualities in candidates:

- The candidate is a good person in general

- The candidate comes prepared

- The candidate is engaging from the initial impression

- Their pay matches up to their talent (certain regions can be very difficult)

- The rep has a big, meaningful WHY that motivates them
- They will open up about who they really are, and what they truly want as a career and for their life
- The candidate does not just want to win the job and the rose, but has the long-term career picture painted

Good People

Good people across the board can mean many things. The person hired should have integrity not only when working, but also in their personal life. The older that I get, the more I realize that word gets around. If you are rude to a neighbor, a waitress, or a secretary, it can get back to you personally or professionally.

An example of this is with a candidate who was doing great through an interview process on Long Island. We will call this candidate Joe. Joe was three face-to-faces and also a field ride in, and was soon about to have his references checked. During this time, the manager spoke with one of their mutual contacts on LinkedIn, also about Joe. It appears that Joe had rubbed this individual the wrong way and was very rude to him. Being as this mutual connection was a close friend of the manager's, his word was trusted. This was not a reference that Joe provided, of course, but it cut Joe right out of the process. All references should be consistent, and the one bad review that was not even a reference knocked him out. His past caught up with him and shows the importance of being a good person across the board.

First Impressions

The best candidate comes to your interview over-prepared. Five minutes early is not early to an interview. Anything less than a full suit and tie, or any less than two copies of a resume and a brag book is just not enough. The handshake should be firm, with a smile and positive, open body language to start off on the right foot. There is research that needs to be done prior to a phone screen or face-to-face interview. This research should be about the company through talking to colleagues, friends, their recruiter - ahem - and the internet. The candidate should have a grasp on the company history. It should always raise an eyebrow when the candidate has questions for the manager that show they have not done any research. Often times, these questions will involve company history, asking about what they will be selling, etc. When these types of questions are asked, the candidate is no longer taken seriously.

Just a month ago, in Houston, there was a field ride set up with a trainer. The trainer conducts rides with reps regularly, and wanted to see how the new hire she would be working with stacked up. The candidate left their home a few minutes early, hit some traffic and was five minutes late. The trainer explained that if you are not on time, early, and prepared she does not proceed. The candidate was not able to attend the ride.

This might seem tough, but I'm sure you don't make it to important sales calls late. *It is completely fair to already have this expectation in place during the interview process.*

Engaging

An engaging candidate is someone who can show off their sales expertise and explain it to you. A true sales rep can create conversation, and build a relationship with anybody, including a prospective manager. This is not a "one and done" interview. If this goes well, there will typically be a series of interviews. The eye contact should be consistent, and a smile is there whenever possible. Engaged candidates will take occasional notes to show interest. They can connect the dots between their current job and the medical device position at hand. Often, they will seek to find common ground. When a mutual contact, town, hobby, sport etc. is identified, it can often create a better bond. At the end of the interview they will close on the next step.

The work history of good candidates should show stability and loyalty, along with numerical and subjective proof of success. They want to show you that they will be on your team for the long haul. Besides their word, what better measure than their prior work history. When a candidate sticks it out at their current role, and the role before that, it shows that they put in the time to be successful. It is rare that people are at companies decades these days, though companies can keep top performers around so long as the work is meaningful to the individual, and the compensation is strong enough. A candidate should be over-prepared with their resume, describing their job functions but most importantly their best rankings, percentages, revenue numbers, etc. in their position. A brag book with the candidate's best numbers, and also with letters of recommendations should be compiled and presented during the interview process.

You are most likely looking for someone who wants to grow with the company, and be there for many years. When on average reps stay for over five years with many companies, it shows that employees are loyal for many reasons. One manager I spoke to envisions himself being promoted, with all of his reps being promoted to trainers and managers. Some reps picture being the top rep in the region, the nation, or being a field manager as their goal, so sticking with the same team is in their cards

The Right Pay

On average, college grads across the United States make $20,000-$30,000, depending on location. This sounds low, but keep in mind college is not a trade school. Most students come out without on-the-job training. I remember graduating school and realizing that what I had really learned is inspiration to go into business (I was unsure of what kind), and the ability to handle life on my own!

Typically, grads are not hired for medical devices roles until they have a year or more of sales experience under their belts. When they do break into a ground-level role, the pay of $55,000-$75,000 sometimes is not enough to satisfy these reps. Usually, this tends to be a regional problem due to cost of living. On the other hand, an outside sales rep a year or two into sales may be exceeding their measures by a large margin if they are paid for their performance. While uncommon, there are reps who are sometimes making $70k or more one to two years out of school.

Pay rate does vary by company, but also by region and even division of your medical company. For example, many large global companies will pay differently and have COLA (cost of living adjustment) for certain markets such as NYC, San Francisco, San Jose, Los Angeles, Chicago, Boston, Seattle, Miami, etc. When hiring in certain cities, the challenge is certainly real to find those who are not seeking super high base pay. It is understandable, but these candidates who are not willing to take the "risk" of having commission be a large percent of their pay are not cut out for medical device sales in the first place. It is often more challenging when you seek large company trained reps in these expensive cities. Some device companies who do not want to pay up to par will end up with inside sales reps, reps trained from smaller companies, or even reps right out of college. You get what the money attracts, so the difference between offering $55k-60k, and $70k can be huge for attracting a much better candidate.

I am often asked for a two or three year outside sales rep in large cities for an associate rep role. This can be difficult when the good sales reps from the large companies are already making this much or more. They need to make this minimum to survive in these cities. Medical device sales is attractive to many, except when it is a huge pay cut for a year or two.

From the recruiter side, we take notes on compensation after each and every call. While we cannot always ask candidates about compensation depending on different state laws, most candidates will volunteer this information because we are trying to help them. Even if the role we talk about does not work for them, we will let them know about future roles since compensation varies.

Big Why

The big why is what gets the candidate up in the morning, bright and early. You want them to have the same desire that you have. The inner drive to be successful. It may motivate them to earn a ton, it may motivate them to help a specific type of patient, etc.

A great example of deep "why's" may be to provide for family. Weddings, bills, family, children, are all expensive, and a stable provider is a huge deal these days. A candidate should be able to articulate clearly and concisely why they want to make money.

Another example of a "why" that is specific to medical device sales is the most obvious: drawing a connection between the devices and saving lives or helping people get better. For example, in an interview a candidate may say that they are interested in selling a product line because, while their current job is stimulating, they would like to not only better their career, but to also help others. If this is a cardiology role, they might mention someone in their family who's had a heart condition, used cardiology devices, or has a heart implant, for example. This clearly demonstrates what motivates this candidate to excel in the role.

Other why's may come from a deep story. Someone may have worked their way through college, grown up working since high school, started a business because they were driven or entrepreneurial from an early age, and been instilled with a great attitude of perseverance and integrity. They may have heard about the company and have a reason why this is the dream company and role for them. Others have role models whose work ethic or success stories have been ingrained in their heads. The deepest motivations need to be thought of prior to an interview, so that the answer to the "why" question can come out and be strong and even moving.

The Real Candidate

Having a candidate open up over the phone or even at a first in-person interview is not easy. The first interview often goes by quickly. If it's under ten or fifteen minutes, it's usually not a good sign for both parties!

Frequently, the first step may be informational and include a standard list of questions. The candidate should reveal as much as they can about their true self, with their best examples and their "why's" to create an open atmosphere. Creating vulnerability and sharing personal stories makes it easy for everyone in the room to open up. This is when commonalities are typically found. Their true personality and authenticity need to shine. The one who comes prepared with their personal stories and deepest reasons as to why they are passionate, what motivates them, and with work and personal examples creates intrigue and interest.

We all know that guy or girl who can light up a room. I do not mean with their appearance alone, but the one with the stories. They seem to draw the crowd in, and have people coming to them because this makes them attractive and magnetic.

Winning the Rose

A great metaphor recently brought up by a close manager was about winning the rose. Even if you do not admit it, you have probably seen reality TV shows on an occasion, or two. I have personally seen some of the Bachelor and the Bachelorette with my wife, willingly of course. The contestants who move on after each round receive a rose. There are usually a few that do not move on and go home with no rose, and some tears. Your ideal candidate needs to be not just looking to win the rose at the ceremony, but to see that the position is long term. It is natural to want to move on, since if you're in sales then you are competitive. Moving onto the next interview round is great, but excellent candidates need to be motivated to stick with the company for the long haul. The rose is not the prize, but a great career in medical device sales is the reward.

National Source Recruiting will help you hit all "lucky seven" qualities you most desire in your new hire!

DISCOVERY CALL

Giving you peace of mind as a hiring manager should be a recruiting agency's number one priority. In addition to delivering on what is promised, the process needs to be seamless, starting with the discovery call. When I speak to a client, I find out about the team and their dynamic. In addition, providing the reason for the opening helps us, and finding out the issue to be solved helps with finding the perfect rep for the position. The opening is obviously costing market share and creating headaches, so it needs to be filled soon. While there is rarely a huge rush to find someone within a week or two, vacant territories warrant another rep covering, or the vacancy will create a steady loss of market share or a lack of support if this is an associate position.

The Perfect Fit

The next step is asking you exactly what you are looking for in your next top rep. The personality traits, background, drive, etc. that you are looking for are very helpful. If you do not know the exact work background that you would like, we suggest some based on the other hires in the company that we have had or have researched.

Job experience is a huge factor here. Someone's path and story to getting where they are professionally is paramount. Where the candidate decided to go to school, if they had hobbies, played sports or worked during school, and their professional journey after graduating are major factors in who that candidate has become.

The examples from earlier about a rep's "why", their ability to be engaging and own the room with their presence, being a good person, etc. are where we can start. In terms of experience, the determination will usually be based on previous successful reps on the team. If you have had success with reps from outside sales because they are more coachable than medical device reps, then you will usually stick to this mold. On the other hand, if this is a high-level sales rep role and the territory needs someone who can come in with expertise in medical sales and make a big splash, it may be better to hire someone already selling devices.

Having experience calling on certain types of physicians is sometimes an important requisite. If you have an opening calling on general surgery and plastic surgeons, operating rooms, etc. you might want someone familiar selling as a rep into these spaces. They would be very likely to jump, and even utilize their existing contacts to be very successful.

When hiring someone with device experience, hiring someone with competitive experience from another company is very rare. There are many reasons for this.

1. Non-competes in the majority of states make it illegal for a rep selling a product line to switch companies and sell the competing product line. In some states it is legal, but typically it cannot be done for a number of years

2. Credibility is lost in the minds of the doctors, surgeons, nurses, etc. that the rep is calling on. If the rep continues to call on the same territory, they will be viewed as someone who switches over and is not loyal. This move makes them look like they are only in the industry to make money and do not really care about which company employs them.

The perfect fit for sales rep or territory manager roles is vastly different from associate positions. The maturity of these candidates needs to be on a different level. This is why it often takes associates a couple years to be promoted. There is a learning process and device mastery that needs to take place. When you are asked what exact experience you'd like to see on a resume, the answer may have to do with tenure, performance, company size, and also industry that they come from.

Current and previous job tenure and stability shows that a rep is very likely stick it out in your role. Their track record is one of the best ways of determining how they will perform in your position. If they have experience in the industry already, then they can use some of their existing contacts to be more successful.

Job performance is a major determinant that you will want to find out about in your next hire. Since you are looking for a top performer for a rep role where you are requiring sales tenure, you deserve to look for reps with a track record. You may ask for someone in the top third, top 25%, or even top 10% at their company. The pay for your positions determines typically what kind of rankings you can command.

Rankings

Rankings set the top reps apart from the rest of the pack and can help your team look great! Quota numbers such as 103% to plan are great, but they do not tell the whole story. If a company has a product that is desirable, had a launch of a hot product or device, or if the benchmark is too low, there is a chance that a good number or even the majority of reps may be over quota. When looking for a top performer, fiscal year-end stack rankings are what need to be brought to the table. So when you ask a rep about their rankings, ask only for year-end rankings. Quarters, half-years or monthly rankings are great, but the year-end rankings show off a top performer. Those with top rankings will be confident in them and know them inside and out.

Brag book

During the interview, expect a brag book. If the rep has great rankings and accolades but no brag book, ask for one. If the rep balks or says it may take a long time, they are blowing steam. A brag book is a binder, or even a folder for newer sales reps with their top accolades. I advise sales reps to put numbers in the front, and qualitative information in the back. All of the candidate's best fiscal rankings, percentages to quota printouts or even screen-shots if the company makes them difficult to attain, should be in the front. For reps that insist these are not provided, there is a small chance this may be correct. But, this means they are likely not in a pure hunter role. They may work in a pod of reps or sell to existing accounts. This is less of a hunter-type role, which may knock them out of the running. When this is the case, then revenue numbers, number of accounts and added accounts might suffice.

The information in the back should be pictures of plaques, trophies, letters and awards. Letters of recommendation from post-college employers should also be in the rear.

What you can realistically find in a candidate depends on the compensation expectations and compensation at-plan for the position. The reputation of the company and how they are doing in the region can also help or hinder this.

Hiring Standards

When working with National Source Recruiting, expect the best throughout all phases of the process. Our goal is not to make a sale or single placement, but to be a partner/advisor that can help you throughout your career. We want to be a resource from start to finish.

From the initial discovery call, until the offer is signed and background check complete, we take pride in being involved as much as you'd have us.

After you see candidates that you like, we assist in scheduling interviews. We send invitations, complete with times and also location if the meeting is in-person. We follow-up after interviews and enjoy manager feedback. Whether or not the candidates move forward, the feedback from you helps the candidate in future interviews, and for us will help to hone in even further on what you want.

Whenever possible, we prepare candidates for each step in the process. Sometimes it is not intuitive for a candidate to come with multiple copies of their resume. It has even happened where candidates, whether told to or not, will not even bring a resume. This should definitely be a strike. Brag books may need to be created for other candidates. For some, they need to be reminded to close. Just because a rep closes day to day in their current sales role, does not mean they will know how to close in an interview.

Frequently, if I do not touch base with a candidate before an interview, they will call me after and say it went great. This is typically the feeling after an interview, which is wonderful! We go over how it went, how they got along with you, the types of questions and their specific answers, and of course their close. A candidate may say the manager was so friendly they expect to move on, but will then say their close was saying "I hope to hear from you" and a handshake. While this is a cordial end to a meeting, there is no expectation of the next step. The candidate did not ask about any reservations you may have, and did not try to secure the next meeting. This is an example of why preparing candidates helps them to be on their game.

For many candidates, this is their first time interviewing since their last job or interviewing in the healthcare arena. In other industries, a softer close or even not closing might fly. But in medical device sales, no close means no deal.

THE PROCESS

Differentiation

When hiring, you expect candidates to come in that fit what we discussed in the discovery call. You expect efficiency and communication from us regularly. When we go to work for you, this is what sets National Source Recruiting apart!

I was fortunate enough to attend a meeting called the First Interview Network in Austin last year. I learned a lot about best practices in recruiting and met numerous other medical device recruiters from across the nation. This was great for learning the new tips in recruiting and growing our business. What I discovered is that many recruiters will receive roles and dish them off to other recruiters, then move on to look for new positions. Our company prides ourselves on working directly on your roles. We go through the tedious sourcing process that does not just include finding resumes of applicants on job sites. While we will occasionally use regional recruiters who I have met over the years, we do source directly on your role.

Sourcing

Sourcing can come from job boards, applicant websites, rosters, and referrals.

Job boards such as Indeed, Monster, CareerBuilder, and MedReps are good, but have been known to cast a wide net. We know that you are looking for a specific fit, and go very narrow whenever possible. The majority of the time, the passive job seeker is not on these sites and has to be reached out to. When I entered the industry, these sites were extremely relevant because LinkedIn hadn't caught on yet. We subscribed to all of them! But typically, we did not find great resumes of qualified candidates on these sites.

For some clients, we have access to the backend and can see all the candidates who apply. We can see the couple hundred (or more) applying for each position. Most of the time, you won't even go through these candidates and will use recruiting agencies like ours. I don't blame you; these are all the resumes that you will find on job boards. Many reps are not even in sales, and some have been out of sales for many years. There are many applicants that apply to every open position and live across the nation from the job location.

LinkedIn is a major force. National Source Recruiting has upgraded Recruiter Corporate accounts to gain access to every person on LinkedIn! Believe it or not, over 40% of the nation is on **LinkedIn: over 133 million people out of the 325 million people in the U.S.**

We have target lists of companies in different industries, from business-to-business to device, to pharmaceuticals, diagnostics, and many others. There are regional companies that took years to identify, and these lists are still growing of course!

When we go through our list of companies after our discovery call, we find those who exactly fit your mold. We send messages, send InMail's, and call all of those who fit the profile.

An InMail is when we message someone we might not be connected with in any way. Usually, we send it after we have already unsuccessfully tried to add them on LinkedIn. We send a message to gauge their interest in the position without disclosing your company name.

Sourcing steps include:

- Calling the resumes we already have of matching candidates
- Reaching out to existing reps and contacts in and around the location
- Calling reps from our lists of candidates in the city
- Asking all contacts we know in the area or nearby for referrals
- Adding reps on LinkedIn from target company lists
- Sending a LinkedIn InMail to passive candidates who are in the network but not our connections
- Cold-calling rosters of companies
- Dialing 1-800 numbers of our target companies
- Making drop-in calls to local Enterprise and ADP offices with the goal of at least a couple of cards
- Working with regional recruiters around the country who have talent pools in specific regions

Meeting the team

Well into the process, the rep will start to meet the team. This can either be over the phone or in person. Sometimes the manager will tell the candidate to do their research and find the other reps on the team and learn more about the job through those reps. This is hard, since not everyone is on LinkedIn. We help with this after the rep has tried on their own and had some success. There are multiple divisions within most device companies, so whenever a lead is found they need to be leveraged to find other contacts.

When reps speak to their potential new teammates, they should have some specific questions to bring to the table. These should include:

- Asking about the day-to-day of the job
- Asking what parts of the job are toughest to learn
- Asking the rep if they have questions
- Moving forward and asking for an endorsement to potentially be their teammate

When speaking to the current reps on your team, the candidate should ask the candidate to ask them questions in return. Nobody likes to be called, asked a laundry list of questions, and then have the call end. To keep this conversational, there should be questions being directed both ways.

A close needs to be implemented at the end. Now, this is not easy because it's not technically an "interview", but the candidate needs to treat it as such. This is not closing them on the next step like in an interview, but asking for their endorsement as their potential teammate. All too often, candidates will call your reps and just ask the basic questions without asking for the endorsement. They will call the rep and go through a couple of questions just to check the box to say that they called.

Post phone conversation with the candidate, your current reps will call you and let you know how sharp and interested the candidate was. They will let you know their recommendation and if the rep should move forward (or not), and if the candidate went in to close them.

PAY

To attract candidates who are passive, we have to be passionate and outline the benefits of a dream medical device job. We definitely do not sell it short. Pitching how beneficial the positions are, how they help people and may be unlike their current field, how they will be improving or even saving lives really catches their attention. Of course, candidates ask about the benefits, whether there may be a car or a car allowance, if any field expenses are paid, and other factors. But the most important feature to a job for many is pay.

When we are telling candidates about device roles, we have a general ballpark of what we think that candidate might be making. Laws have changed in a select few states, and therefore we cannot ask. Luckily, though, when we speak with and build rapport with candidates, they will often volunteer what they are making. There are fourteen states that do not allow an employer to ask about salary history. Though some of the list to follow is restrictive only to government agencies asking about salaries, we still tread lightly since laws are dynamic and do change.

This is a list of the fourteen states that currently have made it illegal to ask about salary:

- California
- New York
- Delaware
- Connecticut
- Hawaii
- Illinois
- Louisiana
- Kentucky
- Massachusetts
- Michigan
- Missouri
- New Jersey
- Pennsylvania
- Puerto Rico
- Wisconsin

Pay is typically indicative of performance. While this is not a gold standard, if someone is in b2b sales for five years with one company and making $40,000 - this is a red flag. It is likely the company does not pay very well at all, but even more likely the candidate is not performing so their commission checks are low. If they are competitive with great numbers to prove it, there is a chance they may be in an inside sales role currently, and these will usually pay less. This goes back to the sections about sourcing and specific job titles that can trick even the expert sourcer on occasion!

When pitching medical device positions, we typically have the advantage that these roles will have better benefits and pay. Most medical device roles will pay a good amount more than the typical outside sales role. Even the associate roles are typically a step up. This is not set in stone, but most sales rep or territory manager roles are uncapped: talk about an attention-getter! It is helpful when you provide our firm with what the top 25% and even the top 10% are making. When we pitch a candidate who is in copy sales for a handful of years and they volunteer that they are making $100k, this helps us tremendously. When we discover we found a great performer with top-20% rankings year over year, we can paint the picture that after they learn the ropes in the device industry and start to get back to the top 20% or better, they can make a significant amount more. It is not that they are underpaid for the industry - that might be great pay for the company and their location. It helps because we can look for roles that pay near or upwards of $100k.

When we discover that they are consistently in the top 25% or better, then we can tell them what the top quarter in a particular medical device role pays.

Generally, you might have an idea of what competitors pay. It seems like it is cyclical or a function of risk to reward. There are companies that are known for very high turnover in the device industry. On the other hand, it is also known that top reps can make $400k, $500k, or even much more division and company-wide. Sometimes this may be only when the stars align, but it is definitely possible.

The pay that candidates breaking into the industry can expect will be in the $50,000-80,000 ballpark for associate roles before benefits, car or car allowance and job expenses.

The pay that candidates who land the majority of territory manager roles can expect is generally $90,000-160,000 before benefits, car or car allowance and job expenses.

Competitor Pay

When pitching medical device positions to a candidate who works for a competitor, it works differently. Generally, and you may be aware of this, there is a sizeable pay range. The base can vary, which changes the compensation at-plan or goal. This is not based on how well they can negotiate, but often on their pay history and performance.

For example, a candidate has worked at a large medical device company for five years and their base has steadily climbed from $55,000 to $85,000 where it is today. In total, they made $185,000 each of the last two years. Let's say that they are interviewing and landed a spot on your team because an organizational realignment with territories at their current company prodded them to look at other opportunities. Their territory was cut in half. While this makes their job easier, their potential to excel is very limited and their anticipated pay is cut to low-$100's next year.

They then have a strong case since they were making a lot more, and your role offers pay of $60k base, and $160k at-plan. They are in the top 25% in their role. In your company, the top 25% make $225,000 or more. The candidate would not be wrong asking for a higher base. Plus, they are also currently employed. This shows that they can juggle an interview process along with their current role, and makes them more marketable. They have been rewarded a higher base in their previous role due to both their success and tenure over five years. Although they will make more in your role if they bring the same performance over, they still have negotiating power.

When an offer is given to the candidate, they most typically will ask for more. If they ask for $90k, there may be back and forth until $75k is settled on.

In my opinion, that candidate is walking into a great position. Their pay potential was cut in their current role and the new position pays performers better. If that candidate walked away due to the company holding firm to the $60k base, the candidate might be missing out. When working with a recruiting agency like National Source Recruiting, you can expect unique perspective from experience when it comes down to pay expectations.

Let's examine both sides here:

Candidate sample points in negotiation:

- Gainfully employed
- May also be pursued by other companies
- Currently has a $85,000 base
- Top 25% performance ranking each year or better

Company sample points in negotiation:

- Top 25% performers make more at this company
- Generous commission potential that is uncapped
- Potential for promotion for top performers

Benefits and Vacation

While it's highly uncommon for candidates to negotiate benefits, vacation is one that is usually included when an offer is sent. Vacation policies may include accrued vacation or may sometimes be granted at say two or three weeks a year where they can take the vacation when they choose.

Upon hire, the candidate usually has a trip or two on the calendar. Often I hear of weddings, honeymoons, vacations, family trips etc. It's usually fair to have a week or two of vacation planned out. I have never seen this <u>not</u> honored unless it conflicts with required training dates, a national sales meeting, etc.

When there is a long leave, extended month or longer vacation planned, or a vacation that conflicts with a set in stone training class, then there are problems.

The training dates need to be discussed during the interview process. When we "lock down" your about-to-be hire about how likely they would accept the offer if extended, we go over any training classes coming up and also ask them about any extended vacations. It is just not worth it for you to go through the entire interview process, send out an offer letter, then find out that a candidate has a two-month family vacation in Europe planned that they already paid for.

Giving Notice

When you hire your new star, you would typically like them to start within a week or two. The standard two-week's notice seems to be old news. Many reps are surprised that when they give notice their employers will have them leave that day, or within a week after finishing a project or training another employee.

But sometimes two weeks' notices do go for two weeks. I've even occasionally had candidates tell me they need to stay on their team for a month before leaving for a new position. In those few instances, those reps did not end up staying for the entire month. When you hire someone and are excited and optimistic about them, you want them on your team as soon as possible!

ADP Hires

Navigating a sales company and locating the proper level of sales reps to fill your role can be complicated. As an example, here is some useful information on the different levels with Automatic Data Processing sales reps. This can be very helpful with sourcing and also working with referrals from this company. Here is the typical pay range and titles of reps that are in outside sales:

- Associate District Managers ADM $50k-$75k

- District Managers DM $60k-$100k

- Senior District Manager SDM $100k-$150k

- TotalSource District Manager- $90k-$200k+

- Sales Executive- $120k-$200k+

- Elite District Manager- $120k+

- Accountant Relationship Manager- $100k+

- Major Accounts District Manager- $120k+

These are just the general income ranges you can expect at ADP. Regionally, they may make more or less. We know that their fiscal year ends in July. At this time of the year, reps are either finishing up their quotas and going strong and staying loyal, or starting to look because they'd like to start a new year at your company potentially.

Base pay at ADP tends to go up slightly when promoted and starts at $52,000. Titles like Account Executive, Sales Manager, Consultant, Specialist etc. mean **inside sales** reps. We do not target these reps for most roles. There are large inside sales hubs in Philadelphia and other locations in Pennsylvania. Paychex, a competitor, has a huge inside sales center in Rochester, where it graduates inside sales reps to outside sales reps. It might seem intuitive that a District Manager is a manager, but it is in fact a rep. A Sales Executive is a manager who manages a team of ADM's and DM's. This is just another example of how varied title names are used.

We have found that the training at ADP is second to few, and the top reps turn out to be successful in most jobs when they leave ADP because of this extensive sales training. Recently, reps have started interning with ADP during school and then make the transition over to Associate District Manager once they graduate.

For Associate Rep medical device roles, it's wise to look at the Associate District Manager and District Manager reps. These reps make in the general range of $50k-$100k, and will bite on Associate roles. When seeking reps on your team with an outside sales background, more doors can open. Three, four or even five-year District Managers with solid rankings might do an awesome job. Accountant Relationship Managers are very polished in their specialty role, and even Elite DM's (those with great rankings) are good finds. TotalSource reps sell a wide variety of offerings with a longer sales cycle, and Senior District Managers have reached a certain level of sales which cannot usually be attained in less than two years.

Across the board, most ADP sales reps have a $550/month car allowance. You have some leverage if your company provides a higher allowance or a company car.

The hierarchy at ADP is logical, but is not easy to understand initially. When it is understood you can often find a hire that will check the box for great sales training background, rankings, quota numbers, etc.

ADP provides comprehensive rankings. Candidates should be taking screenshots of these numbers or compiling them so that they can add them to their ever-growing brag book. ADP documents accounts, growth, and percentage to plan each month and year, so you should not be hesitant to ask for all of their numbers.

HIRING INTERVIEW QUESTIONS

Interviews can be conducted the way that your company mandates, but there is usually room for personalizing both the interview steps and especially the interview questions. Here are some suggested interview questions. They are great to start off the interview, and are very unassuming questions, but can quickly help you tell if that candidate is sharp or is just going through the motions.

- Tell me about a time when you didn't win, and what you learned.
- Tell me three positive adjectives to describe yourself.
- List two negative adjectives to describe yourself and why you chose them.
- Why are you interested in the position and the company?
- Where do you picture yourself in five years?

These questions are usually anticipated by the candidate and have most likely been rehearsed. They are good questions, however, because they can spark a good conversation. Most interviews do not involve twenty or thirty questions, but the questions make way for going deeper into the answers. For instance, for the first sample question the candidate may tell you about a time that they did not land an internship in college. They can spin it positively and talk about how they learned a ton during the interview process. They can mention the specific feedback they received and how they can still hear the interviewer saying it to this day, and have been working to build up in those specific areas ever since.

Everyone should have a personal experience to draw from. For me this was many years ago, but in middle school I did not make the basketball team. I thought I could make any team I wanted to, and had already made high level basketball, baseball and soccer teams with some decent natural talent.

The coach selected me for the "C" team. It truly felt like a C-level team to me after not making the regular team. The team was technically for players 5'3" and under. I felt crushed but played anyways, and then gave up playing basketball after that season. I did end up starting to golf, and then made the high school squad in my freshman year. I can say that I learned from this example, because I realize now I will never quit on something ever again and never have since. I wish I had continued playing basketball and persisted, but I am happy to have walked away learning something from it.

Three adjectives to describe yourself positively is a decent question which will surely be rehearsed. While a candidate will rarely shoot themselves in the foot with this question, they will need solid concrete examples. We prepare candidates to always be "precise and concise" with their answers. They do not need to be brief if they have great details and substance. When a candidate is telling you a story where the details matter to get the message across, they should tell the complete story. If a candidate says they are persistent, this is only a start. They can follow up by saying:

Last week I had an account nearby with XYZ market, one of

my clients in my position at Southern Glazer's. There was a competing rep from Republic National who stopped by the account twice last week. I brought in our new products, new literature, and altered my sales pitch after a meeting with my manager. Instead of losing spirits market share in this store, last week I sold an additional 15 units. I think the persistence that myself and my team put into this account despite competition has made me successful.

This is a recent example from their current position. This is in stark contrast to when a candidate may say "I'm persistent because I never quit, I work very hard, and do not believe a no is a no.". This is a vague answer, and they aren't really telling you anything of value.

The rep may express that they will go above and beyond, and try to finish everything up on their own, and drive themselves crazy, or work too long of hours to complete the job. This can be negative, but you will need a concrete example to prove this because it's too typical of an answer. Better answer examples could be something like this:

"My work requires that I check in at 7:30AM or before at the office to plan the day, take care of a sales meeting if there is one and pick up sales literature. I hit the road from the office before 8:30AM each day to head to clients. After a full day of calls, we are required to come back between 5PM and 6PM each day. Sometimes I will stay at the office until 7PM or later working on tasks that have to be completed to finalize sales or to prepare for the next day. I feel privileged to work for my current company, but I can't let sales or details be incomplete. Last week I was in the office until 8:30PM finalizing some paperwork for a client because to me it was very urgent. I think I need to work on this, not because I want or expect to work 8 to 5 each day, but because I can do better at delegation. I have a hard time letting my contracts be handled by our contracts team, and tend to take them on all by myself. The team is there to assist reps and I really do not use them much. Sometimes I need be better at delegating, since I am not the expert at everything."

For this example answer, the candidate ran you through their work day and sold you on their work ethic. They talked about frequent work examples of them staying late and having a hard time relinquishing control of their contracts because they want to take care of them on their own. At the least, they give a very specific example of a quality that they are working on. The candidate is self-aware and identifies a problem. This shows that they are open to being coached.

The candidate talks about a specific example, and then goes deeper by mentioning the contracts team that should be handling the paperwork to close sales. They are aware that they cannot be a master or all trades, since that is not possible. The candidate demonstrates how they regularly go above and beyond to take care of things and complete sales. They reveal that they are coachable and open to changing their habits because they want to continue growing and succeeding.

The question of why the candidate would like to have this position and work for the company is like a wolf in a sheep's clothing. What seems like such an easy question can trick candidates into giving a "book" answer or a very weak answer. It could be easy to give this answer (which you've probably heard):

I am very interested in working for your company, ABC Medical, because national companies attract me. I saw that your company has been growing and really helps people with your medical devices. I hear that medical device sales is a growing field and I have friends that think I would be good at it

This is an okay answer at best, but definitely not a precise answer that shows a lot of thought. Your candidates should know exactly why they are interviewing for your position. If someone does not know why they are interviewing, or the exact position, it really is a poor reflection on them. They are not specific. They may have done no research to come up with an answer like this. Generalities do not make a great case when compared to this answer:

Your company, ABC Medical, has been in headlines due to the recent launch of your new vascular device, and also because of your recent 10-year anniversary. I saw that your company started by selling a very innovative vascular device that has been updated religiously to both grow ABC Medical and improve patient outcomes. Growth of 5% year over year is strong, and I see a bright long-term future for myself at your company. I would like to be in this position because helping people is wonderful. Currently in my role with ADP, I do help companies with their payroll and HR needs, but do not actually help their well-being. I have seen some of my colleagues from my ADP branch break into competitive companies like ABC Medical, and they are loving it. I spoke to one yesterday who works for XYZ Medical and he told me to look for growing, national companies with solid training, reputation, and a robust product pipeline like yours and this is my first time interviewing. I've been putting my head down at ADP and focusing on success with no distractions and exceeding my quotas. I have been doing my research because I believe this position and find this company to be a great long-term career move for me.

This may be a long answer, but it could be even longer. It is thorough and demonstrates that the candidate has researched your company. The candidate has also done research on your division, has spoken to colleagues, and explains why they may be looking and that they are impressed with your company for many reasons. Often candidates will bring in a personal story about a family member, friend, or colleague being helped directly by medical devices.

These seemingly simple interview questions really aren't simple. A simple answer will not get the candidate very far, and should definitely not impress you. The one- or two-line answers will not cut it. If you really want engagement out of candidates, you can try more specific questions or scenarios. Some of these could be helpful:

- Where do you see yourself ten years down the road professionally?

- Why do you want to be successful with my company?

- What struggle have you overcome in your life that has made you who you are today?

- Have you interviewed for other medical device roles? How does this role compare?

Candidates should draw up where they see themselves within your company down the road. A well-informed candidate will know about the position ahead of them, and even other positions at the company where they see themselves. If another company or industry is brought up, then this is not your long-term hire. Here is a poor answer and also a stellar answer for the question:

- Where do you see yourself ten years down the road professionally?

"I see myself working in the medical device industry in management. I would like to think that if I do amazing in the rep position I can be promoted in a year. I would like to work for a national company"

For this answer, they do not know the career path with the company. They have not been educated about the role through research or by their recruiter. Here is a better phrased answer:

"In ten years, I hope to have been promoted at least two times. I am starting at your company as an associate sales rep. I value the training I will receive, and think it will help me to learn in the field day in and day out and project me to be promoted and then do amazing as a rep.

Down the road, I will hopefully be promoted to a trainer and maybe even a manager just like you. I see myself very fulfilled because I am selling this specific type of medical device, and will be someone who is growing with the company due to putting in hard work and being very coachable"

This second answer shows that the rep understands the career path. They have clearly given the position they're interviewing for some thought, but also know that they can be promoted with hard work to achieve their goals. They have high expectations of themselves, but they are not unrealistic like the first response of being promoted to management in a year.

- Why do you want to be successful with my company?

This is the question where a candidate should talk about the company history, products, and research they have done. In addition to facts you already know about your company, they need to personalize their answer. They need to bring their "why" to the table. A story about how they are motivated because a relative had a certain condition and was saved by a specific medical device, and the reason that they want to make good money is to support a growing family with a new addition on the way shows that this person has the motivation and has no other path but to be successful. It is very smart to choose the rep that has overcome struggle. This should be more than not making a basketball team, or not being hired by a certain company. A great answer should go something like:

"I have an extreme passion for the Diabetes division of your company. It looks like with the ten-year history of your company in this space, and five different and innovative devices, I would be part of a growing division. Personally, in my family I have had a grandparent with diabetes, and my uncle's are a Diabetic and pre-Diabetic. I believe that these devices make a profound impact on many lives, and would be privileged to be part of this amazing team for this reason."

A contrasting example is: "I checked out your website, and it looks like your company has been around quite a while. This division looks like something I'd like because I have been really wanting just to break into a device role"

- What struggle have you overcome in your life that has made you who you are today?

This can be a hard one for the individual who does not know or hasn't thought about why they're fighting and pushing to be their best self. If the candidate can't answer, then they may have nothing really propelling them to be successful. You want the candidate to let you into their childhood, life, and speak about their struggle and how it has shaped them to be successful and how they've learned. An example of a great answer to this question is:

I was fortunate enough to grow up in a home with two loving parents. Both of my parents worked, but they were not always around. My mom was a nurse and still is, and my father worked at the factory across town. I saw my mom work very long and often red-eye shifts, and saw my father each day, without hesitation, leaving before the sun was up with his lunch box, and coming back most evenings when it was dark. I knew that he did not have a passion for assembling washing machines. He carried out his job without fail to put food on our plates. I had the opportunity to attend college, unlike him, and have had so many privileges because both of my parents worked so hard for me. I have the drive to succeed, to make both of my parents proud and wouldn't have it any other way.

A less engaging stab at an answer might be, "I have done well, but never faced anything that I have not overcome. I haven't failed, and have been a winner at everything I have done and just been pretty lucky."

Like it or not, everyone has lost in sports, professionally, etc. at some point in their lives. This person may not have accomplished much because they've taken "safe" job positions or have never really taken risks to be successful.

Do you want the person who just does what's necessary to get by and has never learned from or overcome a BIG obstacle in their lives?

- Have you interviewed for other medical device roles? How does this role compare?

This question does not call for a simple "yes" or "no." It can reveal if a candidate is open with you. If they don't want to speak about the other positions, then who knows what else they do not want to divulge. Transparency is key. Sometimes candidates will speak about the other companies. It can show that they're actively trying to break into medical device sales.

When we speak to candidates, typically the passive ones are the strongest. The reason being, a candidate interviewing currently for four or five roles is overwhelmed. Interviewing is a full-time job. When a candidate needs to take the time to prepare, research, and interview they should not do more than one or two at a time. We have candidates that mix up the companies, products, and even the industries. Here is a sample of a poor answer:

I'm interviewing with two other medical device companies and a pharmaceutical company. I am very interested in breaking into any healthcare role. I just want to help people and all of these companies seem great to me

While the candidate is positive, they cannot speak with knowledge and certainty that there is a difference between pharmaceutical and medical device sales. They have not adequately done their research if they batch them into the same category. They have no specific reason as to why they picked your company, and just want any old medical device role. Do you want someone like this on your team?

This second answer shows that the candidate knows what they're getting into:

I am interviewing with one other medical device company. Stryker Trauma/Ortho has reached out to me and I have had one interview. They have a great reputation in this market from my research, and the compensation is also strong and uncapped. I am highly passionate about breaking into medical device sales, and would rather break into medical device sales with a smaller company like yours. I see the steady growth with your company, and would be instrumental in improving the market share just as I have in my current position with ADP. I really would like to be a part of something growing, where I could expand my career potentially into leadership. I like the idea of getting in early with a company like yours for all of the opportunity.

Here are the short lists of the questions we have gone over. The first list has the simple questions to "warm up," and the second one is where you should expect some great answers because there should be no way around a great answer. (Or better yet you'll know in your gut if it's a great answer or a poor one pretty easily!)

Add your favorite questions to this list. Just make sure the questions you're asking get answers that impress you. You can then be certain you have the right candidate.

Starter Interview Questions

- Tell me about a time when you didn't win, and what you learned?
- Tell me three positive adjectives to describe yourself.
- List two negative adjectives to describe yourself and why you chose them.
- Why are you interested in the position and the company?
- Where do you picture yourself in five years?

Deeper Interview Questions

- Where do you see yourself ten years down the road professionally?

- Why do you want to be successful with my company?

- What struggle have you overcome in your life that has made you who you are today?

- Have you interviewed for other medical device roles? How does this role compare?

TARGET LISTS

To help you with hiring, these lists can be very beneficial. Below are the target lists within specific industries. They include business to business sales and subcategories such as industrial sales, payroll sales, regional companies.

There has been a steady downward trend in the copy and print industry. It's intuitive that most companies are already or at least moving toward paperless for environmental reasons. There is less need for a new Epson or Xerox printer every couple years for this reason. Since the copy rep is becoming more and more rare, we have to be resourceful and find other hunter roles in the other industries which are listed below.

As replacements for the loss of these hunters, Enterprise, for example, provides potential candidates. When you walk into an Enterprise office, the Management Trainees, then Management Assistants, Assistant Managers and Branch Managers generally sell insurance to customers, perform customer service and run the branch.

Account Executives, Account Managers, and those in Fleet Sales at Enterprise do car sales and also prospect companies to sell multiple car (fleet) services or even sell cars directly. Some Account Specialists also do outside sales as a function of their role. The majority of the employees at Enterprise do not perform sales, but knowing the titles of those who do can help you find your ringer. There should also be a search for Enterprise Exotics, a smaller division within Enterprise.

Staffing companies are another target that have helped replace the now rare copy rep. In staffing there are outside sales reps to obtain the job openings from clients (companies). The recruiters work in the office to fill these openings. Targeting the Account Manager (or similar) can help you find hunters that prospect for new openings and are in the field the majority of the time.

The second list below is of lower-paying pharmaceutical companies where we have found reps are well trained, and can provide big sales numbers. To follow the comprehensive sourcing process consistently, each company needs to be checked through with each new opening.

In the pharmaceutical company list, there are contract companies. Contracted pharmaceutical reps do not work directly for the big-name companies like J&J, Merck, etc. They will work through a company like Publicis, PDI, etc. and represent the large pharmaceutical company. The contracts rarely run their full duration, and frequently end without notice for all reps on the contract. These facts make the reps very receptive to direct hire positions. They will have great experience selling but with little job security, making them ideal for the taking.

BUSINESS-TO-BUSINESS (B2B) TARGETS

PAYROLL/INSURANCE:

ADP
Paychex
Zenefits
Paycom
CompuPay, BenefitMall

Heartland Payment Systems
Paycor
Centric Business Systems, Inc
Trinet
Elavon, Inc
SurePayroll
Comdata
Paylocity
Thomson Reuters
Federated Insurance

UNIFORMS:

Cintas

Aramark Uniform Services

G&K Services

Unifirst Corporation

Superior Uniform Group

Superior Linen Service, Inc

Mission Linen Supply

OFFICE/PRINT/EQUIPMENT/BUSINESS SOLUTIONS:

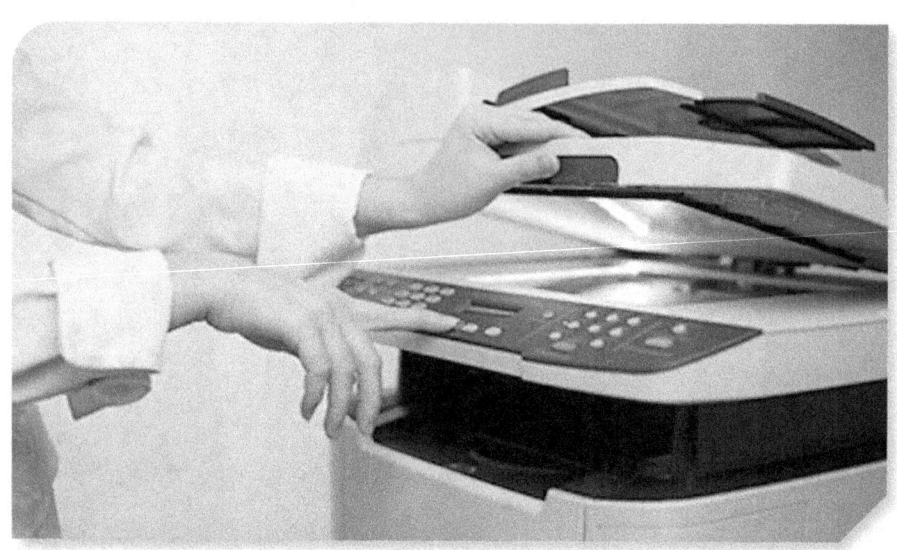

Konica Minolta Business Solutions USA (Copy Tronics)

Canon Solutions America

Toshiba Business Solutions

Atlantic Tomorrow's Office

School Specialty, Inc.

Ricoh USA/Business Solutions (CopyFax)

Advance: We live and breathe this stuff

Xerox:

> (Saxon Business Systems, Zeno Office Solutions, Capitol Office Solutions,
>
> ComDoc, Inc., Amcom, Lewan Technology, Modern Business Solutions, MOTG,
>
> MRC Smart Technology, Dahill, Better Quality Business Systems, XMC, Inc.)

Staples Business Advantage

Pitney Bowes

RJ Young

NovaCopy

IKON Office Solutions

Sharp Business Systems

WB MASON COMPANY

United Business Technologies, Inc.

Humanscale

Interior Office Solutions

Pacific Office Automation

CBS, A Xerox Company

Stewart Business Systems, A Xerox Company

Coordinated Business Systems

Arizona Office Technologies

Zeno Office Solutions

Carolina Business Equipment

Conway Office Solutions

Chicago Office Technology Group COTG

SoCal Office Technologies

SurePayroll

One Workplace

Ohio Business Machines

Unisource Solutions

XANTE CORPORATION

MT Business Technologies

Unison Business Solutions

GFI Digital Inc.
Virginia Business Systems
Atlantic Business Consultants, Inc
Kyocera Document Solutions America

-

FACILITY SANITATION:

Grainger

Ecolab

Stericycle

Ferguson Enterprises

Chlorox

Shred-It

Republic Services

Waste Management

State Industrial Products

Graybar

The Garland Company

CAR RENTAL SALES:

Enterprise Rent-A-Car

Enterprise Holdings

Enterprise Fleet

Enterprise Truck Rental/ Rent-A-Truck

Enterprise Carshare

Enterprise Rideshare

Hertz

Hertz Local Edition

Avis Budget

Penske

Alamo

National Rent-A-Car

United Rentals

CONSUMER GOODS:

Direct Supply
Purina
Nestle
Unilever
Stanley Black & Decker, Inc.
Newell Brands
Colgate Palmolive
Conagra
Proctor & Gamble
RJ Reynolds
Reynolds American
Kimberly-Clark
Ganz
American Greetings
Boulder Brands

CONSUMER FOODS:

The Hershey Company

Advantage Solutions

Sysco

US Foods

Nabisco

Mondelez International

Kraft Heinz Company

General Mills

Kraft

Kellogg

Pepperidge Farms

Hormel Foods

Dot Foods

Dean Foods
United Natural Foods
J.R. Simplot Company
Martin Bros. Distributing Co., Inc.

BEVERAGE/LIQUOR SALES:

Southern Wine & Spirits/Southern Glazer's*

E&J Gallo

Major Brands

The Boston Beer Company

Regal Wine Company

Superior Beverage

Premier Beverage Company

Republic National Distributing Company

Johnson Brothers Liquor Co

Reyes Beverage Group

Terlato Wines

Pernod Ricard

LVMH

Beam Suntory

Inbev

Anheuser Busch

Robert Mondavi

Diageo

Glazer's

Wine Warehouse

North American Breweries, Inc.

Breakthru Beverage Group

Fetzer Vineyards

Jackson Family Wines

Alliance Beverage

Young's Market Company

Monsieur Touton Selection, Ltd.

Constellation Brands

Treasury Wine Estates

Epic Wine Estates

Remy Cointreau

Heaven Hill Brands

Proximo Spirits

Bronco Wine Company

Brescome Barton Inc.

Great Lakes Wine & Spirits

Stand Distributing Co.

Monarch Beverage

Team Promotions

Heidelberg Distributing

LDF Sales and Distributing

Standard Beverage Corporation
Lohr Distributing Company
Grey Eagle Distributors
7G Distributing, LLC
Brown-Forman

TOBACCO SALES:

Altria

EDUCATION SALES:

Pearson
McGraw-Hill
Cengage Learning
Thomson Reuters

STAFFING AND RECRUITING SALES:

Insight Global

Aerotek

TEKsystems

Kforce Inc

Global Technical Recruiters

AccountTemps

Michael Page

Brooksource

Robert Half

Ashton Carter

Maxim Healthcare

Kelly Services

Hays

Tech USA

Bartech Group

Randstad USA

MARKETING SALES:

Hibu

MKTG

News America Marketing

American Marketing & Publishing

RR Donnelley

Dex

MultiView

Clear Channel Outdoors

LOGISTICS & SUPPLY CHAIN

Worldwide Express

Total Quality Logistics

RT&T Logistics

C.H. Robinson

CRST Logistics

Coyote Logistics

XPO Logistics, Inc.

Lawson Products

Landstar

Class C Solutions Group

Schneider National

MSC Industrial Supply Co.

CONTRACT AND PHARMACEUTICAL LIST

PDI

Inventiv Health Clinical

Inventiv Health Commercial

Publicis

QuintilesIMS

Publicis Touchpoint

Avion Pharmaceuticals

Arbor Pharmaceuticals

Braintree Labs, now Sebela

Allergan

Lupin

Eli Lilly

Supernus

Sanofi
AstraZenaca
Teva
Eli Lilly
Takeda
Astellas Pharma
Valeant
Salix
Endo Pharmacueticals

MISCELLANEOUS:

Cumulus Media

ADT

Tom James Company

FedResults

Michelin

Fastenal

SolarCity

3M

Big Ass Fans

Vector Marketing

Air Products

Birch Communications

Marco Technologies

Mosaic North America

SalonCentric

American Red Cross

Power Home Remodeling

AroundCampus Group

YP The Real Yellow Pages

Hilti

Cedar Creek

BDI/Bearing Distributors, Inc

Applied Industrial Technologies

NECESSARY HIRING EXPECTATIONS

You deserve the best talent available on the market that fits your exact standards. There are determinations that need to be made early on in the process about your new hire. Whether you are filling an associate role, sales rep role, clinical position or even manager role, there needs to be a hiring profile. Once you establish what you are looking for, expect top talent!

You may know exactly what you'd like to have. Maybe you've been a manager for five years already, and hired once or twice a year. This adds up to a lot of hiring.

For a sample hiring standard, here is a profile for a sales rep role paying $130k. Let's say this is your standard that has worked very well:

- 1-3 jobs post-graduation
- 4+ years of outside sales or medical device sales experience
- Job stability
- Top 25% rankings or better
- Four-year degree

Knowing these (or determining these qualities) on a discovery call will set the process in motion.

*What you **need to expect** from your recruiting agency, (ahem), or company's talent acquisition team is that they will go to work on **your** profile.*

Candidate flow is key. A couple candidates the first week, and then one per week after that is not candidate flow. You are very clear about your expectations. If the profile can be achieved, we will tell you. If it cannot, we will go through the comprehensive sourcing process to verify this. Sending candidates that fit the five bullets is a given, but expecting a hire out of just a few candidates is not our goal.

You've moved up the rankings, and have the responsibility of hiring and also terminating on occasion. Turnover costs you time that you could be using in so many other ways. Expect your candidates in the interview process to come prepared.

The candidates need to bring their passion and research into the first phone screen through the final interview. Right off the bat, they should know about the products, company, and why they would like to work there. They should be well versed in their work successes, things that they may be working on, and of course know their work history inside and out. Phone screens do nix out a good percent of candidates because these candidates lack the basics.

For face-to-face interviews, expect more out of the candidates than they brought to the phone screen because they are typically in face-to-face sales currently. These outside sales reps will need to bring their energy, great questions, and engagement just like they would to a sales call. In addition, expect a polished resume, expect research to have been done, and expect a solid close at the end for your next interview step. If any of these components are missing, you have every right to not move forward until the star candidate comes along.

Moving to the second time you meet the candidate in a face-to-face, there needs to be more brought to the table. The candidate should engage you more about the products and talk about them in depth, about competitors and what they have found out through research. At this point they should be speaking to other reps within the company, and on your team if you prefer. A competitive market analysis, 30/60/90 plan, or slide presentation will prove to you that the candidate is willing to put in the effort. If they did not bring a brag book to the initial meeting or had one in progress, expect a finished one. There should be printouts of numbers in the front and recommendations, photos of awards, etc. in the rear. All candidates should have a brag book for you by this stage in the interview process.

It's great that some candidates are passive, and just heard about this awesome position through us, but this is no excuse for lack of interview research or preparation. The best hires are those who do not use the excuse that they are currently employed. If they can juggle an interview process and excel in their current role, you know they are both interested and can handle going above and beyond.

If you have a field ride in the interview process, expect engagement. While this step is seeing if the candidate can be a fit, some candidates will not always like what they see while on the job. Some candidates may not be keen on blood, or working with patients, etc. This is good to find out, since you need someone interested in the whole position.

During the field ride, expect the candidate to bring their research and new-found knowledge and ask resourceful questions. Expect them to gain the trust of the other rep in their half or full day of calls and cases. Expect them to close. They are not closing on the job with a trainer or rep on your team, but asking that rep what they would advise to be a strong contender. A rep who shakes hands, parts ways, says "thank you, I hope to hear from you," is not closing at all. The candidate needs to ask for that rep's endorsement to move forward in process. Expect this same necessary close over the phone with each individual your candidate speaks to.

In a less formal setting such as a lunch meeting, expect polish. The candidate should still be dressed like they are interviewing. Expect personal engagement. The candidate who talks all business can't connect with you on a personal level as deeply. Of course, at the end of a lunch meeting still expect a close on the next step in the process.

Expect nothing less than a polished performance in a final. In the last step, it has been weeks or even months of preparation on the candidate's behalf. If they cannot satisfactorily engage in a product role play, talk about the products intelligently, or speak about their current job numbers and successes then they may need reconsidering. Expect even your (or the interviewer's) toughest questions to be answered. There should be no doubts in the candidate's mind that this is the job for them. And there should be no doubts in yours that this is the candidate for the job.

In a final interview, sometimes there is a great emphasis on performance numbers and rankings. We are very adamant a candidate should know their numbers, fiscal rankings, and awards inside and out. For example, if you were speaking to a candidate just one time for an hour before hiring them, would you ask the typical interview questions that they've been asked and gone through four times already in this process or be thorough with their numbers? Sometimes this is the case when a higher-level manager or those in corporate interview a candidate for the final.

Job history and numbers should be clear, with no discrepancies. While not all candidates for this hypothetical position will have top 25% rankings each year, when asked about why they did not hit a top quarter ranking one year, they should have a great answer that does not involve blaming a coworker, boss, or negativity. Sometimes reps are assigned a new territory, given more ground to cover, and other scenarios arise that could explain this.

Expect that the candidate close multiple times on the position. If there is an objection or a wishy-washy response given, you are typically prodding the candidate to close again. This adversity shows how they would address a tough sales call in the field. You would want your new teammate to move forward through obstacles, reservations, and push for the job!

If the candidate does great and accepts an offer, expect that they will go through a background check and complete paperwork in a timely manner. Expect that they will give two weeks' notice or less and then be able to start. There is not a guarantee that your company background check, drug screen, driver's record check, etc. come back clean every time. It's never a sure thing, but is very rare that a candidate will not pass these. Why would someone go through four or more interview steps while knowing they could not pass a drug screen? People look after themselves and value their own time, and that's why this is such a rare case.

Expect communication during the interview process. If you're looking to touch base after each step, we are here to talk about the candidates with you. It is not our goal to push anyone on you who is borderline. We enjoy being a resource and trusted advisor to your hiring. You can have the coordination of phone screens, face-to-faces and all through the final done by us if you'd like. We can be there as much or as little as you need us.

Expect the highest levels of engagement from us throughout the entire hiring process. Period.

HIRING SCENARIOS

Here is a list of ten different hiring scenarios. You will see parallels between your existing hiring process, the difficulties that you've had, and even the successes. This deep dive into applicable interview processes can also be very helpful to candidates looking to break into the medical device industry.

If you are new to the hiring process and looking to expand your team or fill a vacancy, then it might not seem intuitive to use recruiters. The majority of medical device companies use recruiting agencies like ours. If your company does not, it doesn't mean that it isn't a possibility. When we show what kind of value we can add in terms of top performers, efficiency in hiring, and saving you, the manager, and HR time through our thorough and pinpoint processes, we create a strong value proposition.

HIRING SCENARIO #1

One of the clients that we started working with two years ago was in a similar situation. The managers had limited access to agencies. I knew a friend that worked for the company and had moved into management.

He verbalized the pain points. Human resources and talent acquisition were not supplying him with what he was looking for in terms of candidates. There was an existing recruiting agency or two in the mix, but he had a vacancy that was open for three months at that point.

The Tampa market where the vacancy existed had been picked over for months. This was very exciting for us at the time. National Source Recruiting had the opportunity to earn trust, which would ultimately lead to a contract with this company.

At first when we began sourcing on the role, we found that a decent percent of candidates had been contacted. We went very narrow, scrolled through our target list, and the candidate hired (from Insight Global), we reached out sending a paid InMail.

There are many reasons that managers want to switch or even add agencies, including:

- Interviewing the **wrong candidates** has taken up so much of their time that they are fed up
- HR is not supplying enough candidates (candidate flow)
- HR is not supplying candidates who are qualified
- Current recruiting agencies are not devoting the time to send in quality candidates

- Current recruiting agencies are citing the market is out of candidates

In turn, these are just some of the freedoms that you can expect when finding the right candidate and working with a great recruiting firm:

- More time to coach and lead your existing team, attend more meetings, and sell
- More time to help cover the open territories
- More freedom and time after the day is done
- Less obligation to interview candidates that you feel are not even qualified

HIRING SCENARIO #2

At the end of 2017, we began to work with a manager who was recently promoted in a BioSurgery division. I had heard great things about him, and even though he was a new manager he is still someone whose expertise we value. It is awesome to be privileged to connect with these individuals over the phone, and also in person for many managers. Leadership abilities, training and interviewing others on the team and on field rides as a rep or trainer, and their first-hand deep knowledge of the team dynamic are great insights that we like to learn about.

Although he has been part of interview processes before, being the one who makes the decision about the profile for candidates interviewed, the traits desired, steps in the interview process and necessary work experience were new to him.

Not all the details about the candidate were set in stone prior to the Discovery Call. Throughout the call he asked for recommendations about backgrounds of the successful hires we have made. We talked about business-to-business reps, and spoke about a couple of companies that are known for their training. We went deeper into business-to-business categories and decided to go for the true hunter roles.

There are some positions where candidates with a mix of farming and hunting are trained. An example of this is Enterprise. While reps start out in-house, selling insurance and packages and referrals to customers who come to rent cars, many people don't know that Enterprise managers sell on the road. The managers prospect businesses, body shops, and even government agencies to rent or sell fleets of work vehicles.

Enterprise has account managers and sales executives that sell cars all day long.

Some of the categories that produce "hunters" are typically:

- Human Resources, benefits, outsourcing and payment processing
- Insurance outside sales
- Uniform, facilities and workplace sales reps
- Copier sales industry
- Security service sales

He asked about other types of reps that are frequently hired. From our experience, typically for rep roles hires will be medical device reps, and also the top-ranked pharmaceutical reps who don't work in a pod. Pharmaceutical reps are not as frequently hired. The top-ranked reps, who have been promoted, landed President's Club accolades, and just looking for more of a hunter role with a higher earning potential do make the transition successfully in our experience.

After we went to work, the profile narrowed, as this manager wanted someone he believes to be more coachable and from a business-to-business background. There were a couple strong candidates from some of the hunter roles that we mentioned earlier. The process began to weed out even the best medical device and pharmaceutical reps.

This manager was solely advancing the business-to-business candidates. We found a couple more business-to-business reps and then some started to move along in process.

Interview processes vary by manager and company. I have heard of processes involving two steps. Basing a hire on a phone screen and one face-to-face is such a short series of interactions, that most managers and companies will not agree. On the other hand, one client that I recruited heavily for in the past is known for their higher turnover. For this company, though, interview processes were typically ten steps, up to even fifteen. You would think the long process would find the needle in the haystack.

This particular manager was inquisitive about the other managers and the types of processes that are implemented. We went over different examples, the steps, the short processes and the longer ones.

We decided on a process which was about average length for this international Top-20 medical device company:

- Phone screen
- Face-to-face screen
- Deeper-dive face-to-face screen
- Connecting with a couple of reps in the division over the phone
- Field ride
- Phone screen with another manager
- Meeting with the Regional Sales Manager
- Trip to corporate for a series of interviews

This process was VERY thorough, but necessary! If candidates are told they will be in an eight step or longer process, it might not hit home very well. This potentially shows they're not fully committed, but eight steps is pretty long! With that said, some parts are very easily performed from their home, office, car, after hours, etc.

The initial phone screen, speaking to other reps on the phone, and screen with another manager are all over the phone. There are five in-person steps. Definitely thorough, but since the goal is a company, and also a fit for the candidate, it is best to be safe!

The end result of the process was having a candidate who had been in their HR and benefits sales role for four years heading to corporate. We held our breath, since the final interview is a nerve-wracking day. When you have to interview without breaks with three to four people in a row, the fatigue can play tricks on you and even make you second-guess how you did! He landed the position.

HIRING SCENARIO #3

This scenario addresses rolling with the punches. We have discovery call protocols for finding out about new openings and the needs of each client. We have a very thorough sourcing process. This new manager that we started working with six months ago reminded me that customization and flexibility is key!

On the initial discovery call, we established a hiring profile which leaned towards medical device reps or business-to-business reps with a strong track record of top performance. This seemed pretty standard. This manager has been with his company for many years, and had never heard of our company until a couple referrals told him to give us a shot! It threw me off when he said, "Why have I never heard of you?" Well, better late to hear of National Source Recruiting than never.

During this interview process, off we went with a handful of candidates doing an initial phone screen. I touched base after the first round, and heard a couple had done really well. Some were already given the go-ahead directly from the manager over the phone. In that conversation, we went over what some candidates said that he liked. We talked about why some candidates were not moving forward. For the initial phone screen and face-to-face, we always make it a point to prepare candidates, so I mentioned that next time we will make sure the candidates are ready for these types of questions.

That's when I found out that he prefers that we do not prep candidates. I asked him why. The reason is that he wants to see their levels of preparedness and follow-up without being prompted. If we tell the candidate the questions to expect, they can prepare and have super answers. If we do not tell them what they're in for in a screen or face-to-face interview, they have to think on the fly. This is very applicable to when they are working on your team in a challenging position. If they are hired, they need the ability to think on their feet.

In regard to follow-up, we remind candidates to send a follow-up note post-interview. Each step in the process mandates a note to someone. This seems intuitive, since the reps in the field selling send notes to clients frequently. In interviews, though, it's about a 50/50. Some candidates assume that they're moving forward regardless, and some never even think to send one at all.

This manager told us not remind the candidates to send notes or prepare the candidate. What he saw from candidates is all the research they've done, and the level of follow-up and preparedness that no one has helped them with. This is an intriguing way of examining candidates. I do not think he will be the last manager to employ this tactic. When I speak to new managers now in Discovery Calls, I ask what they'd prefer and mention this example. We have stories about top-ranked business-to-business candidates showing up very late, no-shows, not bringing resumes, wearing polo shirts, etc. We want our to reflect that we only send top-notch candidates.

We are not trying to save time by not preparing the candidates as often, but are rather trying to give you a choice. I was privileged to meet this manager a few months back in San Diego. It was a lot of fun, and always a privilege to meet who we are working with.

HIRING SCENARIO #4

This is an example of a passive candidate who started out on the slower side, but then came to bat as the process started to move forward. We had worked with this manager on an open position territory manager role previously, but this vacancy was for an associate rep position. After the discovery call, the manager told us that he was looking for someone who had experience in the industry, or had some business-to-business expertise. We searched for someone with a couple years or more. We went through a couple examples of companies that he liked. He was okay with the normal suspects, and said that adding Enterprise tenured employees could work too.

The reason that we suggested Enterprise is that this position required a rep that lived in or near New York City. When you are searching in the most expensive place in the country, sometimes if you are looking for a two-year tenured business-to-business rep for a $70,000 role, you may come up empty. The successful ones need to make this or more just to make ends meet. Enterprise reps have a mix of sales and customer service in their daily duties, and are paid less because of it.

We put a focus on this profile of some medical reps and then some business-to-business reps. The first couple Enterprise reps that we put in front of him did not cut it. We finally put a rep who we will call Jenny in front of the manager. She had not been interviewing, but had once interviewed for a pharmaceutical job. She had had many promotions with Enterprise, four to be exact.

There is a great difference from the normal pharmaceutical interview process to this process, just as there is a difference in a pharmaceutical job to this job. Besides a difference in what the rep will be selling, pharma is regarded as a softer sale. Jenny voiced that in that interview process her closes were modest. They were more asking permission to move forward than addressing reservations, identifying the next step in the interview process and then closing on that step.

So Jenny went to work to prepare. Jenny had been loyal to Enterprise for nearly three years. Although at Enterprise the managers like herself have to interview to be promoted, and also interview peers, this too is a different interview. They are not automatically promoted, but are asked questions about their ambitions, and what they've learned in their current role within the organization.

This medical device position was going to be more difficult. Jenny knew what she was getting into, and we spoke for half an hour before her initial phone screen. While she was used to some business calls in her Enterprise manager role, she did not know she had to close hard in an initial phone screen. We rehearsed some reservations that the hiring manager may have.

Jenny had her screen, and we touched base with the manager after. It turns out Jenny is pretty good over the phone! She was moving forward. Before we received the location for the face-to-face interview, I received an email that her follow up note was pretty weak. The manager was now on the fence. A couple sentence follow-up note is not the best. We often advise candidates to take notes during a screen, or even a couple notes in a face-to-face interview (as long as they can still pay attention). Jenny lucked out, and was moved forward to a face-to-face.

In the face-to-face interview, she came more ready. Reps at Enterprise work with customers, manage other employees with day-to-day tasks, and also make some sales calls. They also do in-house sales when they interact with people coming in to rent vehicles. She did all of these things, and had an interview itinerary to add to her schedule. She brought a resume that we had worked on, and showed up dressed professionally. At the end of the interview, she had a quick close asking if the manager had reservations, and then asked what the next step is, and finished by saying "I would like to meet you for the next step". The manager said he would let her know. While she did not "lock down" the next step, this was an okay close. The manager mentioned this would not work for a territory manager position.

This time, Jenny wrote a thorough follow-up note addressing a few key points from the interview and expressing her interest in moving forward and the job. She had learned more about the position, and got along well with the manager. She liked his management style, and his track record spoke for itself. He had been with the company for over a decade.

We spoke extensively about the close, as her next step was a deep-dive face-to-face. If Jenny were to succeed here, she would have a field ride, then speak to a few reps over the phone, and then a final.

I advised Jenny to bring something new.

If in each step of the interview process the candidate is not bringing that "wow" factor, and adding new value, you should not move them forward.

While showing up and smiling is a start, for a second face-to-face we strongly advise the candidate to bring a 30/60/90 plan, a competitive business analysis with the product lines or comparing a product to a competitor's product, and of course bring a brag book. Jenny did not have a brag book created. She created a brag book that was a handful of pages. At Enterprise, she did not anticipate leaving until recently, and some of the rankings from corporate are automatically deleted. This can be a problem, so the only way to bring "rankings" would be to bring awards that represent a certain type of finish. For instance, President's Club means top 10% for most companies. At Enterprise there are ESQI scores for the branch which are a percentage. Anything over 90% is an excellent score. Enterprise has Elite Awards and Top Gun awards also. These also mean finishing in the top tier. She printed out these awards, and took a picture of the multiple plaques that she had received. While her brag book was not thick, it had everything she could find.

Jenny brought a 30/60/90 and was specific. This was not a plan where she just stamped the company name on it and brought it to interviews with different companies. This time, she brought the impressive close. There were a couple candidates in process still, and she asked about his reservation. He said she was great, but was not sure she could deal with this job being a "lifestyle", that required grinding, and long hours to become successful. She responded saying that she works most weekends with Enterprise, does not leave work at five o'clock, ever, and enjoys the feeling of accomplishment after a long day's work. She asked if he had other candidates, and he said there were a few others. Jenny did not want to hear "I'll let you know," and asked for his commitment that she would move forward. Very bold.

The manager was impressed, Jenny had his endorsement to move forward. If she did well on the ride and connected well over the phone with the couple reps, she would have her final within a couple weeks.

Jenny wrote a follow-up note. She rehearsed with me what she was going to say over the phone with the other reps. They got back to the manager, raving that she was on-point and had amazing thought out questions. Jenny was open to feedback, had them ask her questions, and her close was second-to-none. She wanted to be their teammate and truly let them know it! The feedback goes right back to the manager, and she treated the conversations accordingly. She also sent follow-up notes to these reps.

Her field ride ended up being a long half-day. She went to three cases with a trainer. These rides were intense, because not only was she in the car with the trainers, three times, then she needed to attend a dinner after work. This a very long time to be on your game. She stayed professional, but also got to know that rep on a personal level. On field rides, occasionally the candidate will not like the product, or will not be okay with calling on hospitals, seeing blood, etc. Jenny was eager, and these elements did not bother her. She sent a follow-up note to the trainer, and took extensive notes. She brought them to the table when she met the Regional Manager a week later.

The culmination of all the preparation, and especially openness to being coached along the way landed Jenny the position! She took the initial feedback about follow-up, about having a much stronger close than they do at Enterprise or in pharmaceutical interviews, and stepped up her weaknesses to her strengths. It took a practice, but she grew sharper throughout each step in the process. Jenny and I spoke a few months ago, and she is enjoying her role and thriving. She is on track to a promotion very soon, and could not picture herself in a more rewarding job.

The interview process is a microcosm of what you see when you work with that candidate.

HIRING SCENARIO #5

This hiring scenario also is about hiring an associate sales representative and the unique challenges that come with it. The manager, who we will call Mack, had hired associate reps and also reps over the years. Mack was not very fond of associate rep hires.

He had hired the wrong associate rep the last two times around. We had been referred to Mack by other managers in this hernia sales division. Mack's experience is that associate reps have not been successful in the last couple years, and he did not seem enthusiastic that he had to hire an associate rep versus a territory manager. Mack told me that he was looking for candidates with that edge, that sharpness, willingness to work hard, and also a track record of about a year or more of outside sales. This was an awesome opportunity. The expectation was promotion in about a year. There was also no relocation and the promotion would be in the same city.

Interviews started in person. As we started to have a couple candidates interview in-person, there was typically hesitancy to move the best candidate forward. I would speak with Mack post interview, and receive pretty strong feedback that he was impressed. Later, the cold feet would set in and Mack would back out and have a reason why each and every candidate would not be moving forward.

Sometimes the field trainer would be present in interviews, and put her feedback in the mix and typically would favor a candidate or two. One candidate even went on a field ride. That rep received the trainer's endorsement to move forward. They were stopped in process because Mack had a concern.

This is a normal concern that we talked about earlier with Millennials. Known for traveling, and valuing new experiences, Millennials like myself are conditioned to shoot for these to best experience life. This candidate had taken time off on three separate occasions during the interview process. Although she did very well in person three times, this made Mack reluctant. Medical device sales are involved, and if she was expecting to take time off right away at the drop of a hat, that was a major issue. This is understandable. We went back to the drawing board, and were sure to screen about vacations that candidates had coming up.

Mack is a great communicator, and we spoke after each round of interviews. It was hard to put my finger on it, but he was gun shy to move candidates because he had made hires that did not work out. While there is no guarantee that any candidate will be a star, we reverse-engineered the hiring of the last reps. They had both worked for small companies. They did not have sales numbers, a strong track record or much documentation of success. Bingo. The profiled had to be narrowed!

Basing a candidate's performance on a track record is king, and so is getting a great feel for him or her in person over a thorough interview process. These last two hires did not have solid track records. They both lacked the large organization training that our most successful associate hires have had. Sure, they can come from any company as long as they are typically in sales, but the hire that hits the ground running usually does come from a large company with great and constant corporate training. When this was discovered, a light bulb went on.

From this point forward, to ease Mack's mind we would only send candidates that worked for larger organizations where there is ongoing training. We would also only send candidates with documentation of strong performance numbers.

Mack started interviewing in person, which is a great way to start out a process. Some managers will want to cut the field down before in-person interviews. Outside sales reps are usually good over the phone, but excel more in person because this is what they do all day!

The first interview morning after this conversation, there were multiple candidates that moved forward. Not only were they on point in person, but they had track records and great numbers to give Mack confidence. Some of the companies they came from were ADP and Southern Glazer's Wine & Spirits.

As the process moved and went to the field ride stage, one candidate separated herself from the others. She had well thought-out answers, a great "why" and pictured herself successful in a long-term career with this company. This candidate was very recently hired, and last she was checked on was doing very well.

Sometimes an initial discovery call can be thorough, but still can't catch everything. Luckily, the deeper details about the other hires came out once the interviews started. Communication here is key. Using Mack's feedback, we successfully found candidates that fit the new mold.

HIRING SCENARIO #6

Sometimes, there are candidates that do not fit the exact mold that is discussed in the discovery call. This is not to say that we look to find alternative profiles of candidates, but after a couple rounds in it can definitely change.

This was my first time working with a manager who we will call Aaron in a Urology division of a large medical device company. He too had an open associate rep position. This role had been worked on by his other recruiter, let's call them his previous recruiter. The candidate flow was dwindling, and he was not finding candidates that would hold their own in the interview process.

We engaged in the initial discovery call for this New York City position. The pay for this position was $70k, so it was not a ton of money for the location but definitely doable. The profile from the call was business-to-business experience of a year or more, ideally medical or pharmaceutical experience. I thought for this pay, it would be very hard to find a healthcare rep.

We have target lists of the lower-paying pharmaceutical and device companies where we can poach reps, but this would likely be a pharmaceutical rep. Associate reps from other companies are typically loyal and are hoping to be promoted readily. We sourced extensively, and found every newer medical device rep and also pharmaceutical rep who had a year up to a couple years of experience. Aaron wanted someone on the up-and-up on their career. He had also come from the pharmaceutical industry.

Phone screens the first few weeks involved a couple pharmaceutical reps, and the rest were business-to-business reps. The B2B reps never seemed to move forward. Only two out of more than ten passed the initial phone screen. One Staples outside sales rep who was ranked number one in the country did get to the field ride. He was checking the boxes steadily, but didn't bring the polish that someone who had broken into healthcare would bring. He also didn't seem to have passion for medical sales. In interviews, this lack of excitement didn't do it for Aaron. This candidate was also interviewing for some other roles in a variety of industries.

Eventually, we could not find anymore pharmaceutical reps. I asked Aaron if inside sales would cut it, and he said sure this could work. We sent a couple of inside sales reps. There was a rep with a background in health and fitness, with a Master's in Exercise Science. This candidate was currently an inside rep for a year and a half, but at a pharmaceutical company.

He had great numbers, and also great excitement. If he had told me that he was an outside rep, I would have believed him. You could tell that he had obviously been in health and had a huge passion for it. Our preparation calls would sometimes go over an hour, and I enjoyed every second of it. I believe that his passion and excitement were what pushed him over the edge. He had never been in face-to-face sales. This candidate had never interviewed for medical device roles before either.

He did his research and created an awesome resume. His marketing plans looked very professional. He checked in after each step in the process, and definitely earned my endorsement. I was hoping he was the guy!

This candidate crossed his T's and dotted his I's with follow-up and bringing value in something new to each interview. In three weeks, he was hired! This was an expedited process because he made allowances to take time off from his current job to prioritize the interview.

The gamble paid off. He was ecstatic to land his new position, and had an optimistic attitude throughout the entire process. The newer associate rep is doing very well in his position. The lesson here shows that being flexible with profile, and suggesting and trying similar profiles gets the job done.

HIRING SCENARIO #7

Truly bringing the energy, enthusiasm and passion into a final interview is definitely huge. On more than one occasion, for roles of various levels, we have seen candidates that do well but not "bring it" in the final interview. For the fortunate ones, there is an additional final, final.

This position was for a new client. It was a $100k sales rep role, and we had a highly promoted Enterprise rep, we'll call him John, who had been there for a handful of years in the interview process. The role was a large step up in pay. This client off the bat requested five or more years in their current position. This position was also in the Northeast, making it even more difficult to find a rep where the pay aligns. But, we never know if it's possible until we source for it!

We went to work. This was for a smaller national company that did have a good name and some great product innovation. We were coming up empty when contacting ADP reps and similar profiles. After five or more years, they were all making much more than the pay for this job. John was very interested in the position, and had a tough schedule with Enterprise. He worked very hard to take time off for interviews. The initial phone screen went well, and his follow up throughout the process was strong and intuitive for him.

Going into the first face-to-face, he had done some research. He didn't know too many of the devices that he would be selling. He got a "did okay" from the manager, and moved forward due mostly to his strong close.

John was a couple face-to-faces in, and was selected to move forward to a field ride. This seemed to give him some motivation. John realized what a high-level role this was. Not only was he helping people all day long, but he was working for a company with a great reputation that was growing. John saw the professionalism of the rep from the ride, and the respect that they got in the field. He wanted to be in this rep's trainer position in a few years.

John was very engaging in the field, and moved onto another face-to-face afterwards. He did fine, as his product knowledge got stronger. John brought a 30/60/90 business plan, and beefed up his brag book for each face-to-face with all the documentation he could find.

The final was coming near. John was moving, and it had been a long process already. He elected to have his final interview a couple hours away where the high-level manager could meet with him. John came prepared, and we spoke in advance for a while. He brought his tried and true documentation, an ability to articulate the products, a summary of his extensive field ride and what he had learned that day in the field. When we caught up afterwards, John said he did pretty well and thinks that his preparation helped him land the job.

I received feedback that they were on the fence with John. This was in an email. I called the manager right away and found out that he definitely had done nothing wrong. There were just a few things that he felt could have been stronger.

They had noted his great preparation and heavy research. John was strong here, and everyone knew it. The problem was, he didn't bring his "A" game in excitement, passion and energy. He had walked in ready to be thorough and close hard, but did not engage the manager 110%.

John did well, but they said they did not feel comfortable that he was the guy. But they did decide to have another final interview. This step would give him a chance to prove the energy that he had for the job.

We did not review his documentation for a second. The coaching involved his body language, and bringing the energy he would bring to a sales call. John was frequently in the field with Enterprise and was a pro at outside sales calls. John talked about his energy in the field, and we had to draw a parallel. I told him that this is an awesome role, and to put it in perspective most of his peers who break into medical device roles from Enterprise will in fact land associate rep roles. Not that these are bad roles at all, but this was an amazing opportunity for him. The pay was definitely there, and he was excited about his field day right after. He needed to bring this energy, and also the perspective that this was a super high-level job for someone with his background.

This second final fortunately gave John another chance. Candidates have final interviews and definitely don't land the job some of the time. This time around, in final number two, John did the energy part right. He brought a confident demeanor into the room. John brought his deep and motivating "why's" to the table, and talked about the field ride in depth. He talked about why exactly these devices would be meaningful to him, and how he was moved during the field ride about having the opportunity to work with healthcare, doctors, and the patients in this hands-on sales role. He expressed what this job would mean to him and his family, and also how it would align with his future goals. This time when he closed, they let him know on the spot that he landed the position. While this is rare, it shows excellence and that he killed it all around.

HIRING SCENARIO #8

During certain interview processes, there can be unorthodox hires. Not every "A" candidate checks all the boxes. Some do not work currently at the large business-to-business companies that we have gone over in this book. For this particular associate rep vacancy, the rep who did amazing in the process was currently not working. This would normally be a red flag for most.

This manager in the northeast we will call Brian. We have successfully worked with Brian a couple times throughout the last two years. He is a newer manager, but excelled as a rep and wants to hire teammates that bring that grind day in and day out. Brian's division of the company has been expanding recently.

With the expansion have been some associate positions opening up. This position just happened to also be in New York City. The pay for this role had been adjusted to $90,000. This seemed amazing for an associate rep role. Once we got to work, it still wasn't as easy as pie.

Brian and I went over the usual suspects. He mentioned that he wanted someone who had great sales training, and could be from pharmaceutical sales but preferably from outside sales. For this competitive of a role, an inside sales rep could not cut it. This associate would be covering New York city, and had to live in the city or nearby and be wanting to work device sales in a great market with unlimited potential.

Brian was looking not for a one-year sales rep, but two years minimum. I knew that if we sent him a candidate that had had two or three jobs in the last two years it wouldn't cut it. We went to work and found what we thought were some good candidates. They did well, but did not bring that fire, that spark.

In the interview, Brian would talk about how the job has its huge upsides. He would tell candidates how grinding and hustling will get the job done, but it is going to be a lifestyle. Some candidates in the process were scared of this work/life balance. We often get calls from candidates looking to exit outside sales or even pharmaceutical sales due to work/life balance. If they are calling us about medical device sales positions, we steer them to other fields. Generally, if you are in sales and successful and working 9-4 or 9-5, you aren't at the top of the pyramid.

These types are not putting the time in. Some business owners are in first thing in the morning, and others need to meet after hours even over dinner to get the contract signed. Brian made this expectation clear. Although many associate rep roles will entail that reps have many overnights a month, this New York city role did not have that many. The traffic and amount of potential business in the area was staggering.

A few weeks in, a candidate who had an ADP background and I spoke over the phone. I thought he worked there currently, so I was bummed to hear over the phone that he had left six months ago. He left to pursue real estate and that venture was not working out. He was back on the job market. I knew that the lack of job stability may hurt him, but we pushed him forward to Brian anyway.

The candidate seemed eager on the phone. Of course he was, though, since he was a job seeker who was not employed. His polish really shined through in the first phone interview and face-to-face. His tenure previously at ADP for just short of 2.5 years and great performance numbers brought him to the top. This candidate went through the process in just over two weeks. The reason for this was that he had time to make allowances, but was also doing great at each step in the process...

I was so thankful that Brian overlooked the move to real estate AND that the candidate was not currently employed. While profiles for your candidates are entirely up to you as a manager, sometimes there will be a profile that could eliminate great hires such as:

- Being 100% set on the candidate having one or two jobs since graduation
- Needing the candidate to be currently employed in outside sales
- Requiring promotions in their current role

Occasionally companies have one level of sales representative. If candidates are coming from Enterprise or ADP, you know that they should have a promotion or two if they are successful! For companies such as Paychex and Xerox, reps can stay reps with great numbers for a long time. They may still have no promotion and it could take a handful of years to be promoted to even a trainer position.

HIRING SCENARIO #9

Even the toughest of vacancies can sometimes be filled with the sharpest business-to-business reps. Although relationships and experience calling on doctors or hospitals really go a long way, sometimes there is no replacement for a hard worker in the interview process who goes the extra mile.

This hiring scenario highlights how an outside sales rep can be great for the long haul. They often bring to the table the qualities of being very coachable, moldable, and still have a thorough track record. These candidates you can picture on your team growing and improving each year. It helps also because they are not typically as far along into their career and could potentially be at your company for many decades.

Often times, it can be tempting to select the internal associate rep or a medical device rep. This story is about how even the most selective of managers will pick a strong outside sales rep for high-level positions.

This Midwest role was a full rep role. I received a call from the manager whom we had worked with before. This was for a newer division of a large device company. The division was growing, but slowly because it is in a tight sector with a lot of competition.

While the division had been growing, there were only a couple products that the rep would be selling. This is a role that would be a grind, where the consultative sales rep who is used to a VERY tough selling environment would be an awesome fit.

We had the discovery call. The manager had a great open perspective, asking for a mix of tenured medical device reps with a track record and only the pinnacle of high-performing business-to-business reps. For a role that paid in the mid-$100's at-plan, they needed to be ready to perform and hit it from day one.

Interviews kicked off with a mix of both profiles. Frequently, the medical device candidates with a few years of experience with previous business-to-business backgrounds are awesome. They have relationships and experience selling devices, and are used to the grind, and bring the hunter-mentality from their outsides sales position also. There were two device reps of this profile in process, and a couple business-to-business reps.

After the first phone screen and face-to-face date, just three reps were moving forward. Usually there will be a couple half days of interviews for the first round. It just so happened that after the first day one of the surviving candidates would go all the way.

The interview process would not be a cake walk however. We will call the B2B star John. John had two medical device reps to contend with, and a late challenger was an internal candidate. While we did not have a ton of intelligence on this candidate, they were currently in an associate rep role and interested in relocating and interviewing for this position for a faster promotion to sales rep.

These device reps are polished. They have been heavily trained on calling on doctors, working long hours, calling on hospitals, and had great numbers. They were both doing well in their current positions, but looking for a global company where they could be rewarded more financially.

When I prepped both device reps, they did not need much and were very polished. John had been loyal to one job since college. He was a copy sales rep, and he had steadily increased his percent to quota year over year for the last five years. John had only interviewed for a healthcare sales role one time. We had to rehearse before each step.

When you find out that candidates are only interviewing for one position, it is a great sign. Sometimes, they will need to do a great amount of research and prepare with their recruiter a lot. It is worth the time. On the opposing side, when candidates are interviewing for many roles it increases their chances, but at the same time they will struggle to keep their current numbers up and will also have a hard time investing into any one interview process.

John took the time and memorized a large amount of product information. He did not use notecards in the interview. The manager said that the way John rattled off the information was amazing. It was mostly correct, and John accepted some feedback moving forward on how to better sell the products. If he could sell copiers in a declining industry, he definitely could also do well here was the theory.

John learned about every single product throughout the process, identified the competitors and learned about them, and how others on the team sold the product. He created presentations for the interviews, and outworked the device reps. One of the device reps told me prior to his second face-to-face that "he had a good feeling this one's in the bag." The device rep spoke too soon.

While confidence is amazing, being cocky and too sure before you close something can jinx it! John capitalized and brought his hard work and research and findings from the field ride to the next interview. He was given the go-ahead from the manager to head out to corporate. John is still doing well on this team, and exemplifies how with the right attitude and the ability to go above and beyond, a business-to-business candidate can outpace just about anyone.

HIRING SCENARIO #10

For this final example of hiring, there was a hold in the interview process that threw a wrench into things. These holds are infrequent, and can run for a few days, up to months or more. The hold in this case went into place a couple days before the final interview.

Our vacancy was in the Carolinas. A very cordial candidate from Enterprise had run the gamut. Michael was actually up against a couple of his colleagues and a few outside sales reps for this position. This associate rep role paid $60k, and required a grind and great intensity plus overnight travel. Michael was no stranger to the lifestyle, and worked most weekends in his sales and management position of Branch Manager.

Michael was promoted three times in his role. When we spoke initially, we talked about future advancement. It was known that with Enterprise, most advancements will earn them $5-10k more. This was a steady and modest increase every year or so. When I told him how helpful the devices were in hernia surgery, he was already interested. What pushed him over the edge was the fact that when promoted, the sales rep may make $100k more than an associate rep.

Michael squared off and carried out the initial phone screen and face-to-face. A couple reps were moving forward. He was the candidate on point with closing, follow-up, and brought to the table about the best rankings and awards that an Enterprise rep could have. Michael took the assessment for the company and did fine.

He finally met the manager one more time, and was signed off and also given pointers about what to expect with the Regional for his final interview.

We touched base, and he contacted other reps and researched products, competitors and best selling practices. Michael had his final on the calendar for a week out. The next day, he was given a call from the manager that his position and all associate positions were on hold. While holds and layoffs are very common in the pharmaceutical industry, it took us by surprise. There was no end date known for the hold.

We would just wait to hear back, and Michael planned on checking in every few weeks. Just one week later we received good news. The manager told the Regional that this was "the candidate", to please push him through and it had worked! Michael performed in his final and was the exception to the hold. These holds are very rare, but to break through the hold was an anomaly.

RESOURCES

Hiring Checklist

Here is a hiring guide with recommended lists that cover the basics. Please use these and customize them over time to fit your needs.

About Your Opening

- Territory covered
- Reason for the opening
- Frequency of expected overnight travel
- Relocation expectation
- Base, commission at-plan, the amount top performers could make, benefits
- Current market-share, potential upside for a strong rep
- Potential for promotion

About Your Hire

- Desired personality characteristics
- Background type, (i.e. business-to-business sales, medical device sales, medical device cardiology sales, pharmaceutical sales etc.)

- Years of desired experience
- Number of jobs post-graduation
- Specific companies you prefer them to come from
- Specific industries you prefer them to come from
- Other specific requirements you think would make them successful

About Your Process

- Initial phone screen, face-to-face interview, or even corporate personality assessment. Determine which kicks off the interview process
- Estimated number of face-to-face interviews
- Research expected from the candidate about competitors, marketing plans, and reaching out to current reps to build rapport and gain knowledge
- If there is a field ride
- Lunch or dinner interviews to determine how the candidate performs in a less formal setting
- Interview with other managers, trainers, reps or high-level manager if applicable
- Final interview (can be a panel, with you, with a high-level manager, corporate interview)
- Optional interview with HR depending on company
- Anticipated start date
- Background check
- New Teammate!

About your Recruiter

- Let you determine the background and qualities of your new hire

- Engage in a discovery call if you would like it

- Stay in communication

- Provide steady candidate flow

- Be as hands-on as necessary with coordination and preparation. Thoroughly leave no stone unturned in sourcing

- Prepare candidates so they will do their research and impress you

- Ensure that if an offer is given the candidate is prepared to accept

End Matter

Writing a book about some of the best things that I've learned in the recruiting industry has been challenging for me. It has helped me to better learn my craft, and has also made me realize what I do is all for "good people." My company is privileged to work with hiring managers from reputable companies, and additionally the candidates who are the future of these companies.

I would be more than happy to steer you in the right direction for your staffing needs. If my agency National Source Recruiting can help, I'll tell you. If we cannot, I'll also tell you and we can send you in the right direction.

"Believe in what you are doing and in those who are helping you do it and you are bound to win"

- Napoleon Hill

www.ingramcontent.com/pod-product-compliance
Lightning Source LLC
Chambersburg PA
CBHW070321240526
45468CB00025B/1388